CIRCULATION AND WATER PROPERTY VARIATIONS IN THE NEARSHORE ALASKAN BEAUFORT SEA

Thomas J. Weingartner
Stephen R. Okkonen
and
Seth L. Danielson

Institute of Marine Science
University of Alaska
Fairbanks, AK 99775

June 2005

Final Report

MMS Contract 1435-01-00-CA-31083

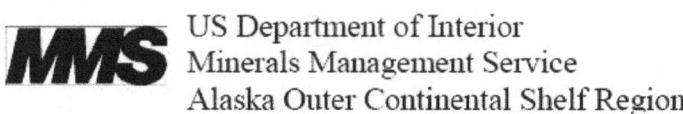

US Department of Interior
Minerals Management Service
Alaska Outer Continental Shelf Region

CIRCULATION AND WATER PROPERTY VARIATIONS IN THE NEARSHORE ALASKAN BEAUFORT SEA

Thomas J. Weingartner
Stephen R. Okkonen
and
Seth L. Danielson

Institute of Marine Science
University of Alaska
Fairbanks, AK 99775

This was funded by the U.S. Department of the Interior Minerals Management Service (MMS), Alaska Outer Continental Shelf Region, Anchorage Alaska, under Contract No 1435-01-00-CA-31083, as part of the MMS Alaska Environmental Studies Program.

May 2005

LIST OF FIGURES

ABSTRACT

Three years of current meter and water property data were collected year-round (1999 –

2002) from the landfast ice zone of the nearshore Alaskan Beaufort Sea. The data show large

seasonal differences in the circulation that is defined by the set-up and breakup of the landfast

ice. During the open water season (July – mid-October) mid-depth currents often exceed 20 cm-

s^{-1}, whereas during the landfast ice season (mid-October – June) these currents are generally <10

cm-s^{-1}. Tidal currents are feeble (<3 cm-s^{-1}) year-round and probably do not play a dynamically

significant role on the inner shelf.

Most (>90%) of the current variability is in the along-shore direction year-round. For the

most part, mean currents are not statistically different from zero over the whole record or in

individual seasons. Open water currents are significantly correlated with the local winds, but

currents beneath the landfast ice are not. Calculations conducted over both seasons suggest

along-shore sea-level gradients are about 10^{-6}, with the magnitude of these gradients being only

slightly larger during the open water season than during the landfast ice season. These gradients

are presumably set-up by the winds during the open water season, but their origin during the

landfast ice season is unknown. During the open water season upwelling-favorable winds force

westward flows that are strongly sheared in the vertical and with maximum currents at the

surface. In contrast, downwelling favorable winds are weakly sheared in the vertical. The

symmetry is presumably to the strong stratification associated with upwelling winds.

Cross-shore flows are generally small (~3 cm s^{-1}) compared to along-shore currents.

However, cross-shore flows of ~10 cm-s^{-1} were observed during the landfast ice season when the

spring freshet resulted in an offshore spreading of a buoyant plume beneath the landfast ice.

Although measured cross-shore flows are generally small, satellite imagery suggests that frontal instabilities associated with low-salinity nearshore plumes can transport inner shelf waters offshore to the Beaufort shelfbreak during the open water season. Observations from elsewhere in the Arctic suggest that cross-shore current speeds associated with instabilities can be as large as 30 cm s^{-1}.

The results suggest that oil spilled beneath the landfast ice will stay within the vicinity of the oil spill source as current speeds will rarely exceed the threshold velocity required to transport an oil slick once it has attained its equilibrium thickness. Because of the broad spatial coherence in the flow field (at least 30 km in along-shore extent), underice currents could be monitored at one point and transmitted real-time to cleanup crews in the event of an underice spill. This information would verify the current speeds and whether oil would stay in the vicinity of the spill. Oil spilled during the open water season could be rapidly dispersed over great distance in both the along- and cross-shore directions, however.

Water properties also vary seasonally in response to ice formation and melting, the spring freshet, and wind-mixing. Salinities increase and temperatures decrease throughout the winter due to freezing and brine expulsion from sea-ice. During the spring freshet, the inner shelf is strongly stratified and remains so until the ice retreats and winds mix the water column. The annual suspended sediment cycle, based on transmissivity measurements, suggests rapid deposition of river borne sediments beneath the landfast ice during the spring freshet, with re-suspension and transport occurring throughout the open water season depending upon storm frequency. Re-suspension and transport is also vigorous during the formation of landfast ice and we conclude that much sediment is incorporated into the ice matrix at this time of the year. Ice-incorporated sediments are either transported with the ice or returned to the water column during melting the following summer.

There are several important issues that we believe need to be addressed in the future. Modeling of the landfast ice zone requires an understanding of the role that ice-water friction plays in this region. This is likely influenced by the unknown, but complicated, underice topography. Second, the source and magnitude of the along-shore pressure gradients responsible for the underice currents needs to be determined. Third, it is not clear if the findings based on current measurements made in water depths ≤ 12 m apply to deeper portions of the landfast ice zone. Hence the cross-shore coherence in the underice circulation field needs to be determined. Fourth, the introduction of freshwater creates stratification that can lead to an asymmetric current response to wind-forcing during the open water season. Observations on the thermohaline structure of the Beaufort shelf are needed in order to understand and model the circulation field during the open water season. Cross-shore salinity fronts, established by river runoff, can become unstable and cause energetic cross-shelf flows capable of carrying pollutants far offshore. The dynamics and kinematics of these features need to be explored to properly include them into ocean circulation models. Fifth, sediments can adsorb pollutants; hence we recommend that consideration be given to the potential role that ice plays in the transport of sediment on this shelf

I. INTRODUCTION

The nearshore zone (here defined as the portion of the shelf between the coast and the ~20 m isobath) of arctic shelves differs substantially from their mid- and low-latitude counterparts because of unique geomorphologic and climatological attributes. Arctic shelf tides are generally weak and rivers empty directly onto the shelf rather than into bays. Thus, the nearshore effectively functions as an estuary, insofar as it serves as the transition and mixing zone between the Arctic's terrestrial and marine environments. Climatologically, the large annual cycle in air-sea heat exchange and freshwater runoff cause enormous seasonal variations in the buoyancy and momentum fluxes to the shelf. For example, more than 90% of the annual river discharge from arctic rivers (defined here as rivers whose watersheds lie entirely north of the Arctic Circle) occurs over a brief period in early summer. (For larger rivers, such as the Mackenzie or Lena, approximately 90% of the annual discharge occurs between June and September.) Much of this discharge occurs before the landfast ice has completely retreated. Landfast ice is a unique characteristic of most arctic shelves. During the winter months it is anchored to the seafloor out to the 2 m isobath [*Reimnitz*, 2000] and can extend offshore to between the 20 and 40 m isobath [*Reimnitz and Kempema*, 1984; *Macdonald and Carmack*, 1991]. In contrast to drifting pack ice found over the outer shelf and basin, landfast ice is virtually immobile. On windward shelves, such as the Beaufort, its offshore boundary is highly deformed when pack ice collides with the landfast ice edge. On lee shelves, such as the Laptev Sea, the offshore edge of the landfast ice is typically smooth and terminates at the edge of a polynya. The landfast ice extent varies among arctic shelves; it extends ~100 km offshore in the East Siberian Sea [*Morris et al.*, 1999] but is of much smaller extent, and in a few places even absent, on the Chukchi shelf. Because it is effectively immobile, landfast ice inhibits the transfer of momentum from the wind to the ocean and therefore drastically influences arctic shelf dynamics. Moreover, it probably reduces communication between nearshore and outer shelf waters where the wind stress is transmitted efficiently to the ocean. As will be seen the landfast ice effectively determines seasonal conditions on arctic shelves.

Herein we report on year-round measurements of currents, temperature, salinity, transmissivity and fluorescence (which provide qualitative measures of suspended load and chlorophyll, respectively) obtained from moored instruments in the Alaskan Beaufort Sea. The primary goal of the program was to assess the magnitude of underice currents in the vicinity of Prudhoe Bay where offshore petroleum development activities were planned or underway. These measurements were needed to guide response procedures in the event of an accidental oil spill beneath the landfast ice. Laboratory studies indicate that oil slicks at equilibrium thickness and in contact with immobile, smooth ice begin to move at current speeds ranging from 3 cm-s^{-1} for low viscosity oils to 7 cm-s^{-1} for high viscosity oils [*Cox and Schultz*, 1980]. Threshold velocities increase to 15 - 25 cm-s^{-1} as the underice roughness increases.

Previous current measurements in this region yielded contradictory results. *Aagaard's* [1984] measurements suggested that current speeds seldom exceed 10 cm-s^{-1} in the landfast ice portion of the Beaufort Sea, while *Matthews* [1981] inferred that speeds of up to 35 cm-s^{-1} were possible at least occasionally. Both studies were of relatively short-term duration, however with instruments moored close to the seabed. The velocity measurements reported here were collected by bottom-mounted acoustic Doppler current profilers (ADCPs) over a three-year period (August 1999 – September 2002) and represent 9 instrument years of data from beneath the landfast ice zone. Although the geographic scope of the program was limited, the results provide a firm basis for regional oil spill response planning. In addition, they provide a look at this unique marine environment and raise a number of questions pertinent to the physical oceanography of nearshore arctic shelves influenced by landfast ice.

The outline of the report is a follows. Section II provides background information on the Alaskan Beaufort Sea shelf. The field program is described in Section III and the results presented in Section IV. Section V explores some of the possible influences of freshwater runoff on the oceanic dispersal of any contaminants introduced at the coast. Conclusions and recommendations are summarized in section VI.

II. THE REGIONAL SETTING

The Alaskan Beaufort Sea shelf (**Figure 1**) extends ~500 km eastward from Point Barrow to the Mackenzie portion of the Beaufort Sea shelf in Canadian waters. The shelf width is ~80 km as measured from the coast to the 200 m isobath. Shelf depths grade smoothly offshore with bottom slopes typically being ~10^{-3} inshore of the 100 m isobath.

Sea ice can cover the shelf year-round, although more typically the inner shelf (and in recent years the entire shelf) is ice-free during the summer months. Landfast ice begins to form in October and extends 20 – 40 km offshore through mid-June. It covers approximately 25% of the shelf area [*Barnes et al.*, 1984]. The landfast ice is relatively smooth adjacent to the coast, but is increasingly deformed offshore. Maximum ridge intensity and height increases moving seaward, and the magnitudes of both variables increase through winter [*Tucker et al.*, 1979]. These parameters can also vary along-shelf and it appears that the landfast ice zone on the Mackenzie shelf is much less deformed than on the Alaskan Beaufort shelf [*Tucker et al.* 1979]. Ice keels form beneath the ridges and can gouge the seafloor [*Barnes et al.*, 1984] and form piles of grounded ice, stamukhi, along the seaward edge of the landfast ice. The stamukhi appears to be important in protecting the inner shelf (and landfast ice) from pack ice forces [*Reimnitz and*

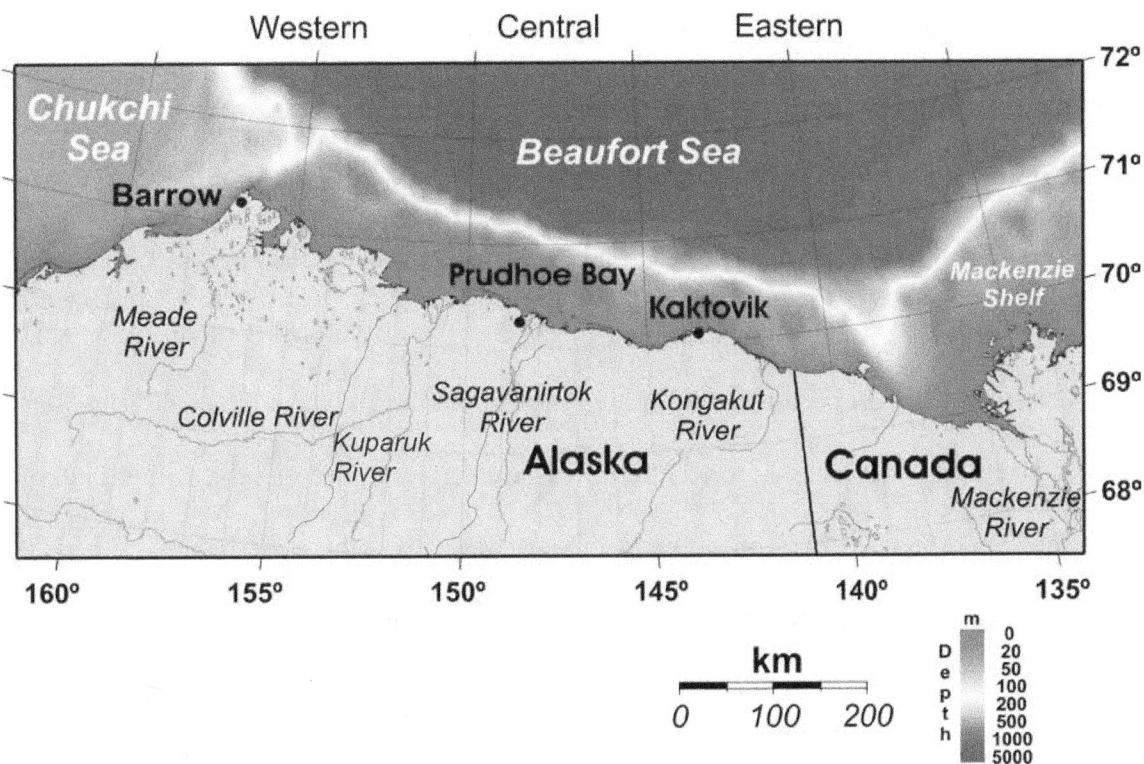

Figure 1. Map of the Alaskan Beaufort Sea and North Slope with place names and subdivisions indicated.

Kempena, 1984] and on the Mackenzie shelf provides an effective barrier to the exchange of dilute nearshore waters with saline offshore waters [*Macdonald and Carmack*, 1991].

Ice deformation and stamukhi formation is related to the northeasterly winds over the outer shelf. Northeasterly winds prevail from fall through spring and force pack ice into the landfast ice edge. In summer, weak westerly winds blow over the southern Canada Basin [*Furey*, 1998] although several strong westerly wind events typically occur each summer and fall along the Beaufort coast as low-pressure systems propagate from the Bering Sea [*Maslanik et al.*, 1999]. Seasonally varying mesoscale winds may substantially alter the synoptic wind field over the nearshore zone, however. For example, a persistent summer sea breeze results in mean westward winds within ~25 km of the coast [*Kozo*, 1982a, b]. *Brower et al.* [1988] indicate that mean summer winds are easterly, which suggests there is a reversal in wind direction on crossing the shelf. From October through April mountain barrier baroclinicity [*Kozo*, 1980; 1984] can produce along-shore divergence in the wind field. This effect occurs when the southward flow of low-level cold air from the Arctic Ocean is blocked along the northern flank of the Brooks Range. The resulting isopycnal slopes induce eastward surface winds of $O(15 \text{ m s}^{-1})$ over a horizontal width scale of 200 – 300 km. The western Beaufort coast is rarely influenced by the mountain barrier effect because it lies more than 300 km north of the Brooks Range, but the eastern Beaufort coast lies within 60 km of the mountains. Consequently, winds can be westward over the western Beaufort coast but eastward along the eastern coast. *Kozo* [1984] estimated that the mountain barrier baroclinicity effect occurs ~20% of the time during winter.

Three distinct oceanic regimes bound the Alaskan Beaufort Sea. To the west, waters of Pacific Ocean origin flow northward from Bering Strait and across the Chukchi shelf. While this flow divides along three main branches across the Chukchi shelf, the one most relevant for the Beaufort shelf is the outflow through Barrow Canyon in the northeast Chukchi Sea [*Mountain et al.*, 1976; *Aagaard and Roach*, 1990; *Weingartner et al.*, 1998; *accepted*]. Variability in the canyon outflow flow is large, especially in fall and winter, and mainly due to fluctuations in the regional winds [*Weingartner et al.*, 1998; *Weingartner et al.*, accepted; *Woodgate et al.*, accepted]. Some of the Barrow Canyon outflow continues eastward as a subsurface current (or slope undercurrent) along the Beaufort shelfbreak and slope where it forms the upper halocline waters of the Canada Basin [*Mountain et al.*, 1976; *Aagaard*, 1984; *Pickart*, 2004; *Pickart et al.*, accepted]. Presumably some of the water exiting Barrow Canyon rounds Pt. Barrow and continues onto the inner portion of the western Beaufort shelf, although no measurements have been made here to examine this issue. The outer shelf and continental slope provide the offshore boundary for the Alaskan Beaufort Sea. In the upper 50 m or so the flow is westward and part of the southern limb of the wind-driven Beaufort Gyre. This flow can occasionally be reversed by strong westerly winds and/or by occasional shelfbreak upwelling that advects eastward momentum from the slope undercurrent onto the shelf at least as far inshore as the 50 m isobath [*Aagaard*, 1984; *Pickart* 2004].

The Mackenzie shelf joins the Alaskan Beaufort shelf to the east and it is likely that, at the very least, the eastern Beaufort shelf is influenced by the year-round discharge from the Mackenzie River [*Carmack et al.*, 1989; *Macdonald et al.*, 1989; *Macdonald and Carmack*, 1991]. Mackenzie shelf water has been detected throughout much of the Canada basin, including the continental slope of the Chukchi and western Beaufort Sea as far as 160°W longitude [*Guay and Falkner*, 1998; *MacDonald et al.*, 1999a]. It thus seems likely that wind- driven currents transport Mackenzie shelf waters onto the Alaskan Beaufort shelf as well. In this regard, we note that the migratory behavior of arctic cisco provide indirect evidence for the intrusion of Mackenzie River waters onto the inner shelf of the Alaskan Beaufort Sea. These fish apparently require a nearshore band of low-salinity water in order to complete their annual migration between the Mackenzie and Colville rivers each summer [*Colonell and Galloway*, 1997]. The migratory corridor is presumably maintained by the westward drift of low-salinity water from the Mackenzie shelf. In addition to the Mackenzie River, a large number of smaller rivers discharge into the Alaskan Beaufort Sea (**Figure 1**). These are asymmetrically distributed with most of them discharging into the central and eastern portions of the shelf. This asymmetric discharge, along with the influence of the Mackenzie, might establish an along-shelf density gradient that gives rise to an along-shelf baroclinic pressure gradient.

Our measurements were made in the vicinity of Prudhoe Bay, which lies about midway along the Alaskan Beaufort coast. Although a number of smaller streams empty into this area the three major rivers (and their watershed areas) that discharge into the study region are: the Sagavanirktok River (4800 km^2), the Kuparuk River (8100 km^2), and the Colville River (53,500 km^2). Only the first two of these are routinely gauged, and only seasonally, because the gauges are installed at breakup and removed in fall prior to freeze-up. The discharge time series for the two USGS gauged rivers are shown in **Figure 2** for each summer during which ocean measurements were made. (The spring freshet in summer 2002 was not detected as this occurred earlier than normal and prior to the installation of the gauge.) The annual discharge cycle is characterized by a rapid initiation and increase in runoff in late May or June that lasts about 2 weeks during which time nearly 90% of the annual discharge occurs. Following this spring freshet, the discharge is small and gradually decays to negligible values by October, although the decay can be punctuated by smaller, shorter-lived and sporadic discharge events following summer rain storms. The Colville has a similar seasonal cycle, although the discharge is substantially larger because of its larger drainage area. Unlike the Mackenzie and other large Arctic rivers, there is no measurable winter discharge from any North Slope rivers as most freeze to the bottom and all have watersheds lying entirely within drainages underlain by permafrost..

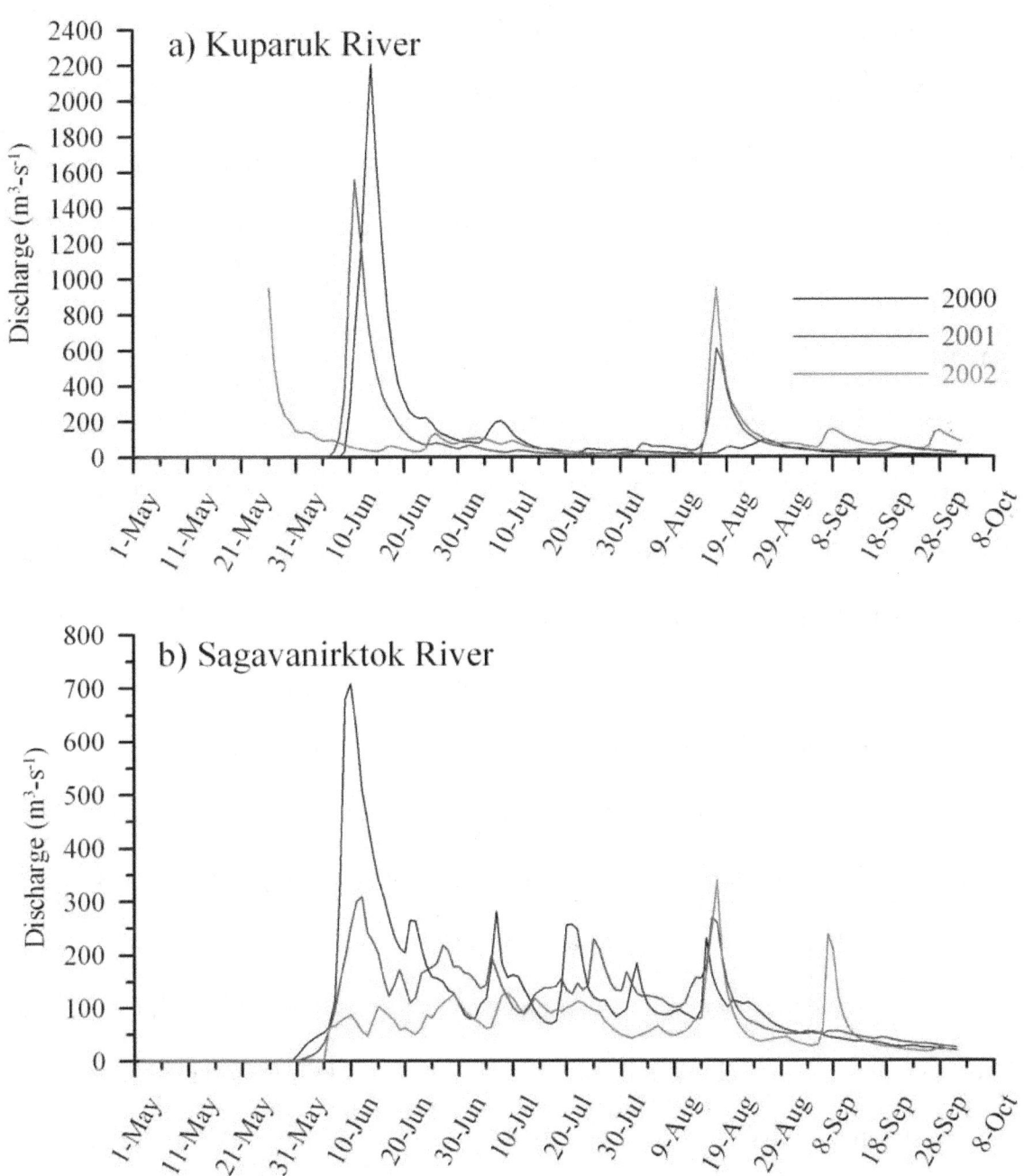

Figure 2. Daily runoff for a) Kuparuk and b) Sagavanirktok rivers in 2000, 2001, and 2002. Note that the spring freshet in 2002 occurred prior to the installation of the gauges. The Sagavanirktok River gauge is located about 140 km inland from the coast so the discharge at the coast is probably greater than that measured by the gauge.

III. METHODS

The data set described below comes from four oceanographic moorings deployed (**Figure 3**) in

Stefansson Sound and adjacent waters where present (Northstar Island) and future oil development efforts are targeted. The area provides important habitat or is a migratory route for a variety of fish, birds, and marine mammals, including seals and bowhead whales. Of particular concern is the potential influence on the unique Boulder Patch kelp community in Stefansson Sound [*Dunton et al.*, 1982], which lies near the Liberty oil development prospect in the eastern portion of Stefannsson Sound. Moorings ARGO, DINKUM, and McCLURE were deployed in late summer or fall of each year beginning August 1999. Because we were uncertain if moorings would survive drifting ice in this shallow (<10 m) environment the mooring deployments in these years took advantage of partial protection afforded by a widely-separated chain of barrier islands and shoal, which lie 15 – 20 km offshore. In the final year (Sept. 2001 – Sept. 2002), we felt confident that our mooring design minimized ice damage risk and so we deployed the REINDEER mooring in 12 m of water offshore of these islands. All moorings survived except the 2001 deployment of McCLURE, which was demolished by drifting ice 8 days after deployment. (Although all of the instruments were recovered, the data are unusable for our purposes, except for the pressure record.) To the best of our knowledge the data presented here are the first year-round records from the nearshore zone of any arctic shelf.

Velocities were measured from either a 1200 or 600 kHz ADCP set in a gimbaled collar and mounted onto a mooring frame constructed from plastic angle stock (**Figure 4**). The gimbaled mount insured that the ADCP remained vertical even if the frame tilted from the horizontal by 20° or less after deployment. (Observations made during recovery dives indicated that frame tilts were always negligible. Moreover, the ADCP tilt sensor indicates that the instruments remained level throughout the deployment.) Ancillary instruments (Seabird, Inc.,

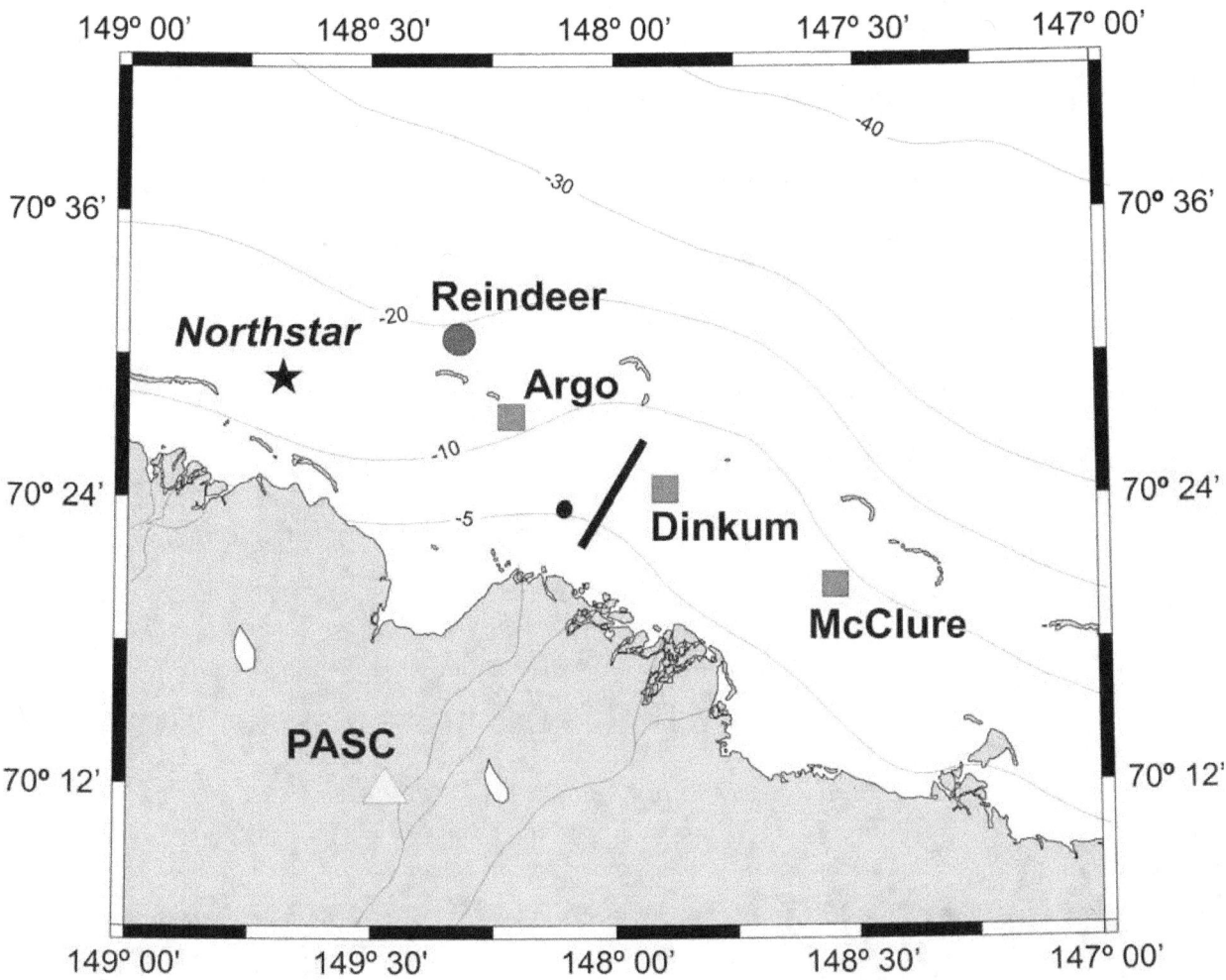

Figure 3. Location map showing current meter moorings and the PASC weather station in Deadhorse. Moorings ARGO, DINKUM, and McCLURE (red squares) were deployed in each year from summer 1999 – summer 2002, while REINDEER (blue square) was deployed from summer 2001 – summer 2002. Northstar is a production island constructed in 2000 and 2001, while the McCLURE mooring lies within the undeveloped Liberty field. The solid line through DINKUM indicates the approximate location of the June 2000 CTD transect. Depth contours are in meters.

MicroCats and/or SeaCats, with at least one mooring containing a strain-gauge pressure sensor) were fastened to the legs of each frame (**Figure 4**) and inclined to the vertical. At some locations the SeaCats included a transmissometer and in the last year a fluorometer. The inclined mount has no effect on the temperature and salinity measurements, however, the transmissometer lens might have collected settled sediment on occasion. We will note these possible biases when discussing the data.

The mooring positions, sensor packages, and bottom depths at each mooring site and for each year are listed in **Tables 1 – 3**. The MicroCats and SeaCats were re-deployed after the first year without a post-calibration (performed by the manufacturer) while freshly calibrated instruments were used in the final year. Based on pre- and post-calibrations and comparisons with the winter T/S relationship along the freezing point curve we estimate that the salinity values are better than 0.1. (Salinity is evaluated using the practical salinity scale and is thus unitless.) The salinity record at mooring ARGO was erroneously high throughout the 2000 – 2001 winter and is not used. Hourly wind speed and direction were obtained from the Deadhorse airport, denoted as PASC in **Figure 3**.

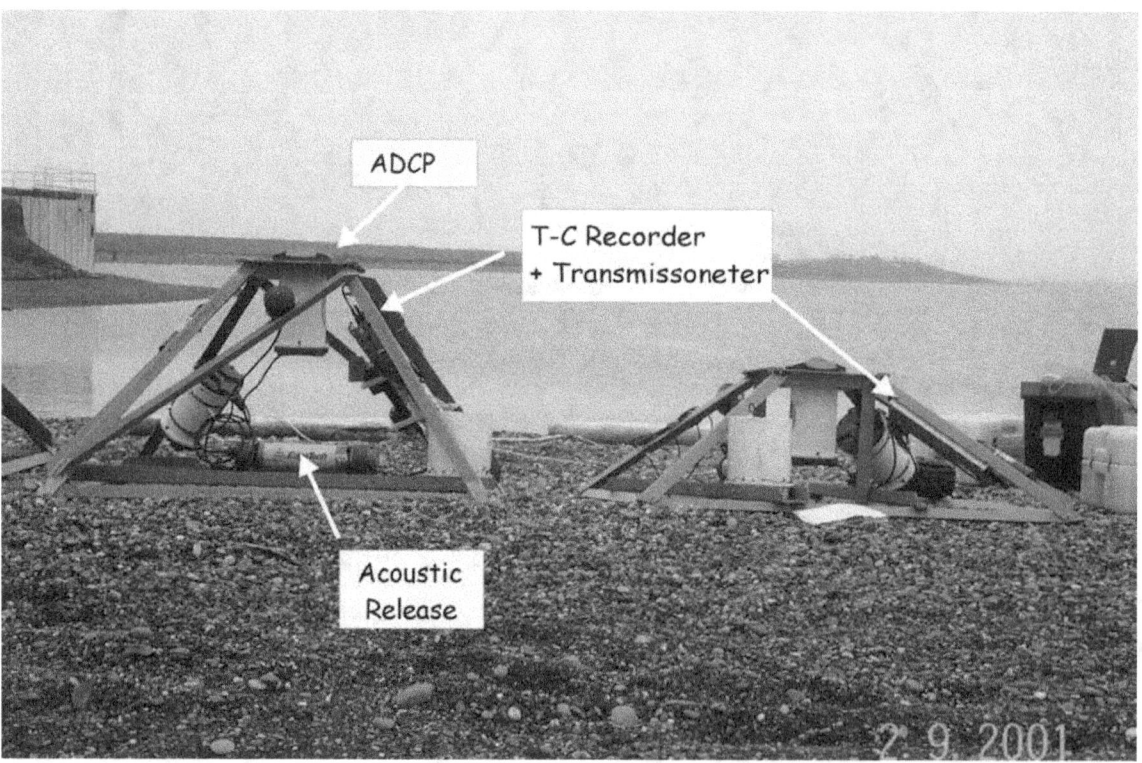

Figure 4. Photograph of the PVC mooring frames with various instruments used in the study.

Table 1. Mooring Specifics for Data Analysis Period 2200/14/AUG/1999 - 2100/31/AUG/2000

Mooring Name	Latitude (°N)	Longitude (°W)	Instruments	Variables Measured	Bottom Depth (m)
ARGO	70° 27.177'	148° 12.722'	1200 kHz ADCP MicroCat	Water Velocity Temperature Salinity Water Pressure	8.4
DINKUM	70° 24.352'	147° 53.656'	1200 kHz ADCP SeaCat	Water Velocity Temperature Salinity Transmissivity	6.8
MCCLURE	70° 20.204'	147° 32.701'	1200 kHz ADCP SeaCat	Water Velocity Temperature* Salinity*	6.7
PASC	70° 11.7'	148° 27.7'	Anemometer	Wind Speed and Direction	

- McClure SeaCat data of 1999-2000 unusable because of instrument setup problem.

Table 2. Mooring Specifics for Data Analysis Period 2200/3/SEP/2001 - 1700/19/AUG/2002

Mooring Name	Latitude (°N)	Longitude (°W)	Instruments	Variables Measured	Bottom Depth (m)
ARGO	70° 27.172'	148° 12.666'	1200 kHz ADCP MicroCat	Water Velocity Temperature Salinity* Water Pressure	8.8
DINKUM	70° 24.371'	147° 53.632'	1200 kHz ADCP MicroCat	Water Velocity Temperature Salinity Water Pressure	7.3
MCCLURE	70° 20.164'	147° 32.700'	1200 kHz ADCP SeaCat MicroCat	Water Velocity Temperature Salinity Water Pressure Transmissivity	7.6
PASC	70° 11.7'	148° 27.7'	Anemometer	Wind Speed and Direction	

*ARGO salinity record in 2000-2001 not used because of sediment/biofouling and calibration problems.

16

Table 3. Mooring Specifics for Data Analysis Period 2200/2/SEPT/2001 - 1700/18/AUG/2002

Mooring Name	Latitude (°N)	Longitude (°W)	Instruments	Variables Measured	Bottom Depth (m)
ARGO	70° 27.168'	148° 12.654'	1200 kHz ADCP SeaCat	Water Velocity* Temperature Salinity Fluorescence	7.6
DINKUM	70° 24.371'	147° 53.632'	600 kHz ADCP SeaCat	Water Velocity* Temperature Salinity Transmissivity Fluorescence	6.8
MCCLURE	70° 20.164'	147° 32.700'	1200 kHz ADCP SeaCat	Water Velocity** Temperature** Salinity** Water Pressure Transmissivity** Fluorescence**	7.2
REINDEER	70° 30.539'	148° 19.212'	1200 kHz ADCP	Water Velocity*	12.7
PASC	70° 11.7'	148° 27.7'	Anemometer	Wind Speed and Direction	

* Bottom Track data on all ADCP instruments for this 2001-2002 was not collected. Water velocity data is good.
** McClure 2001-2002 mooring hit by ice 8 days into record and most data not usable. Pressure data is good.

IV. RESULTS

1. Sea ice, currents, and winds

Before presenting the record length and seasonal statistics, we describe the seasonal cycle of currents and ice thickness for each year from the DINKUM mooring (**Figures 4 -6**). Sea ice thickness, H_{ice}, was estimated from ADCP data as the difference between the bottom depth, Z_b (**Table 1-3**), and the sum of the height of the transducer above the bottom, H_T, and the range from the transducer at which the intensity of the reflected acoustic signal was maximum, R, (e.g., $H_{ice} = \{Z_b - [H_T + R]\}*1.12$), where the factor 1.12 is the ratio of the sea water density to the sea ice density. There is an uncertainty in the thickness estimates of 0.5 m because the ADCP integrates return signals over a 0.5 m depth bin. This error occasionally introduces high-frequency noise in the data which was eliminated by smoothing the ice thickness time series with a 5-day running mean. Sea ice forms in early October, gradually thickens to ~1.7 – 2.2 m by mid-March, and then remains constant through mid-June. Ice then melts rapidly and disappears by mid-July. The seasonal asymmetry in ice growth and ablation rates occurs because new ice forms on the underside of the ice with the freezing rate decreasing exponentially with H_{ice} [*Maykut*, 1986]. By contrast, ablation primarily occurs at the surface and proceeds rapidly once the surface snow cover melts or the surface is covered by low-albedo, silt-laden waters from river overflow [*Dean et al.*, 1994; *Searcy et al.*, 1996].

Unfiltered velocity time series from the uppermost bin (bottom-track velocity; U_{BT} in the figures) are large and noisy when the surface is ice-free, but negligible once landfast ice is established. (A programming error in the final year's deployment voided the ice-tracking capability on the ADCPs. Instead of using U_{BT} to indicate the onset and end of the landfast ice period we used the large seasonal reduction in current speeds to approximate the dates of landfast ice formation and retreat in this year.) The abrupt transition in U_{BT} allows unambiguous definition of the open water and landfast ice periods in each record. The data suggest that in each year landfast ice is present from mid-October through the end of June or the beginning of July, while the open water season (including drifting ice) spans the July through mid-October period. Thus landfast ice is present about eight and one-half months. The figures also show time series of the current shear, $d|V|/dz$, (where $|V|$ is the speed and z is depth) between the shallowest depth bin beneath the ice or sea surface and the deepest depth bin. At the DINKUM mooring the depth range over which these differences are computed varies ~4 m during the open water period to ~2 m during maximum ice thickness. Current speeds typically differ in the vertical by ≤ 4 cm s^{-1} when ice is present, but can exceed 40 cm s^{-1} during the open water period. The bottom panel in each plot shows the unfiltered time series of the velocity component projected onto the principal axis of variance (listed in **Tables 6 - 8**). These indicate that the largest current speeds and variance occurs when landfast ice is absent. This seasonal scenario is repeated in all three years among all moorings. **Table 5** lists the dates of landfast ice set-up and break-up for each year and mooring based on analysis of the ADCP data sets.

Table 5. Landfast ice set-up and breakup dates and times for each year and mooring.

Landfast Ice Setup Date												
	Argo			Dinkum			McClure			Reindeer		
Year	1999	2000	2001	1999	2000	2001	1999	2000	2001	1999	2000	2001
Month	10	10	10	10	10	10	10	10				10
Day	15	20	13	15	22	13	15	22				10
Hour	0	3	12	0	16	10	0	16				15

Landfast Ice Breakup Date												
	Argo			Dinkum			McClure			Reindeer		
Year	2000	2001	2002	2000	2001	2002	2000	2001	2002	2000	2001	2002
Month	6	7	6	6	7	6	6	7				6
Day	30	4	30	30	2	23	30	2				27
Hour	23	18	1	23	5	23	23	0				14

Figures 8 - 15 are time series of the low-pass filtered (35-hr cutoff) major and minor velocity components, demeaned (over the deployment period) sea-level, and the wind stress components based on Deadhorse winds for each mooring are shown for the landfast ice (**Figures 8 – 11**)and open water (**Figures 12 – 15**) seasons. Visual inspection suggests that the current components along the principal axes are highly correlated with one another and this is confirmed through empirical orthogonal function (EOF) analysis (based on the correlation matrix) whether calculated over the whole record or separately for each season. The results for each deployment (**Table 5**) show that the first mode accounts for ~90% of the variance, while the higher modes

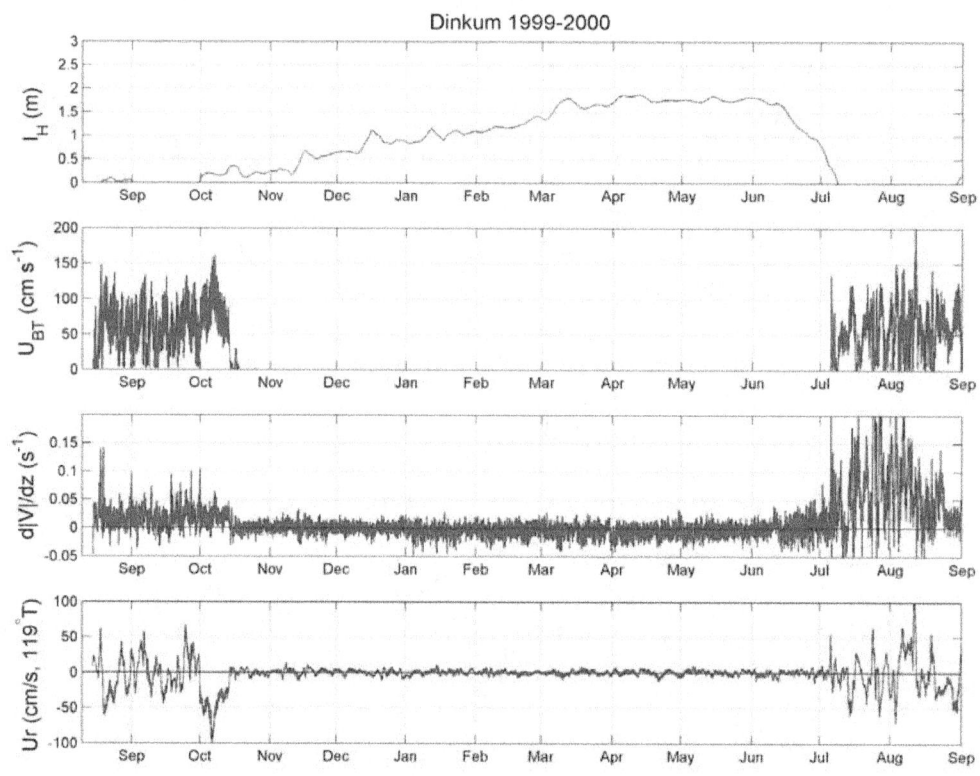

Figure 5. Time series of (from top to bottom) ice thickness, bottom track speed, shear, and velocity along the principal axis of variance at DINKUM for the first deployment period (1999 – 2000).

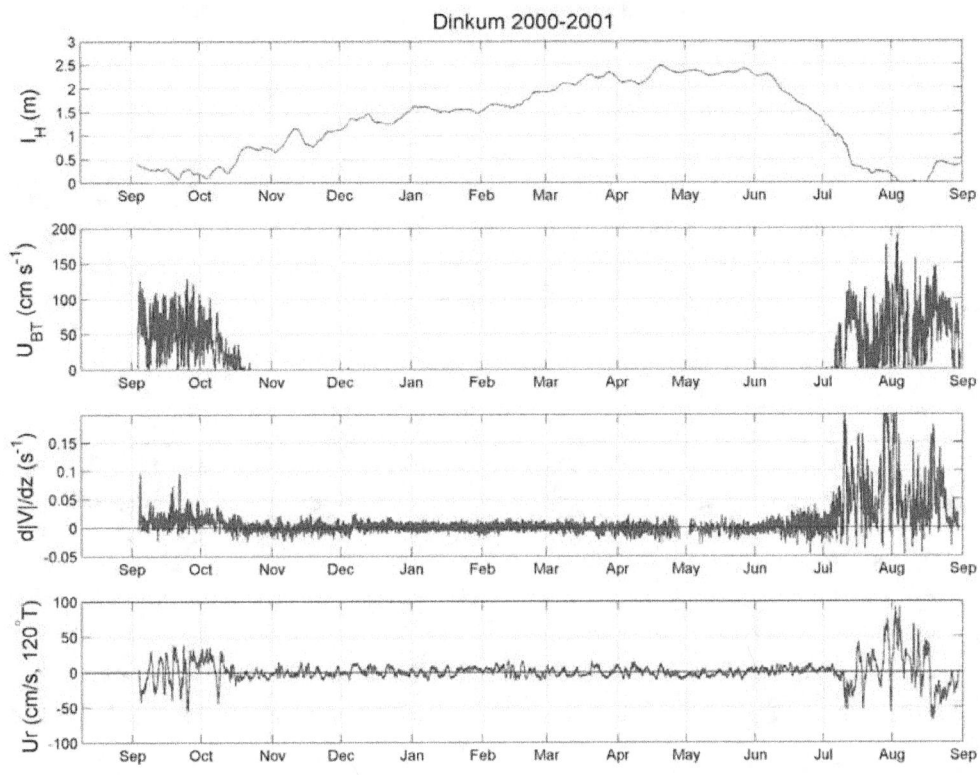

Figure 6. Time series of (from top to bottom) ice thickness, bottom track speed, shear, and velocity along the principal axis of variance at DINKUM for the second deployment period (2000 – 2001).

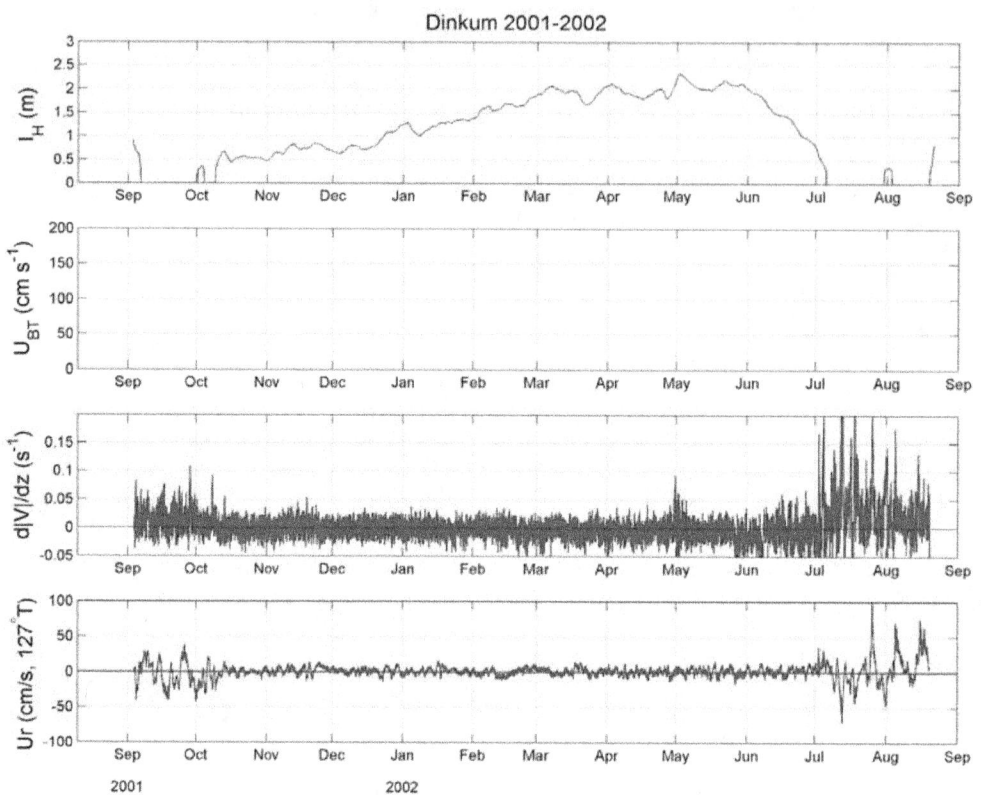

Figure 7. Time series of (from top to bottom) ice thickness, bottom track speed, shear, and velocity along the principal axis of variance at DINKUM for the third deployment period (2001 – 2002). A programming error voided measurements of the bottom track velocity.

are not significant based on *North et al.*'s [1982] criterion. The dominance of the first EOF

implies that flow variations in this region are coherent over spatial scales of at least 30 km so that

a single mooring could be used to capture the local along-shore flow variability. Although this

finding is not surprising given the simple bathymetry of the area, it was not clear at the outset of

the study that these scales should hold in the presence of landfast ice because complex underice

topography could generate velocity variability over small horizontal scales and thus degrade

spatial coherence. There might in fact be seasonal differences in the velocity de-correlation

scales because of the landfast ice, but if so these scales are larger than 30 km. Indeed the

reduction in the variance explained by the first EOF mode during the 1999-2000 landfast ice

season relative to later years could be due to differences in underice topography, although we

have no means to examine this possibility.

Table 5. Percent variance explained by the first empirical orthogonal function for velocities
projected along the principal axis of variance.

Period Analyzed	1999-2000	2000-2001	2001 – 2002
Landfast	77	90	94
Open Water	93	94	93
Whole Record	95	93	93

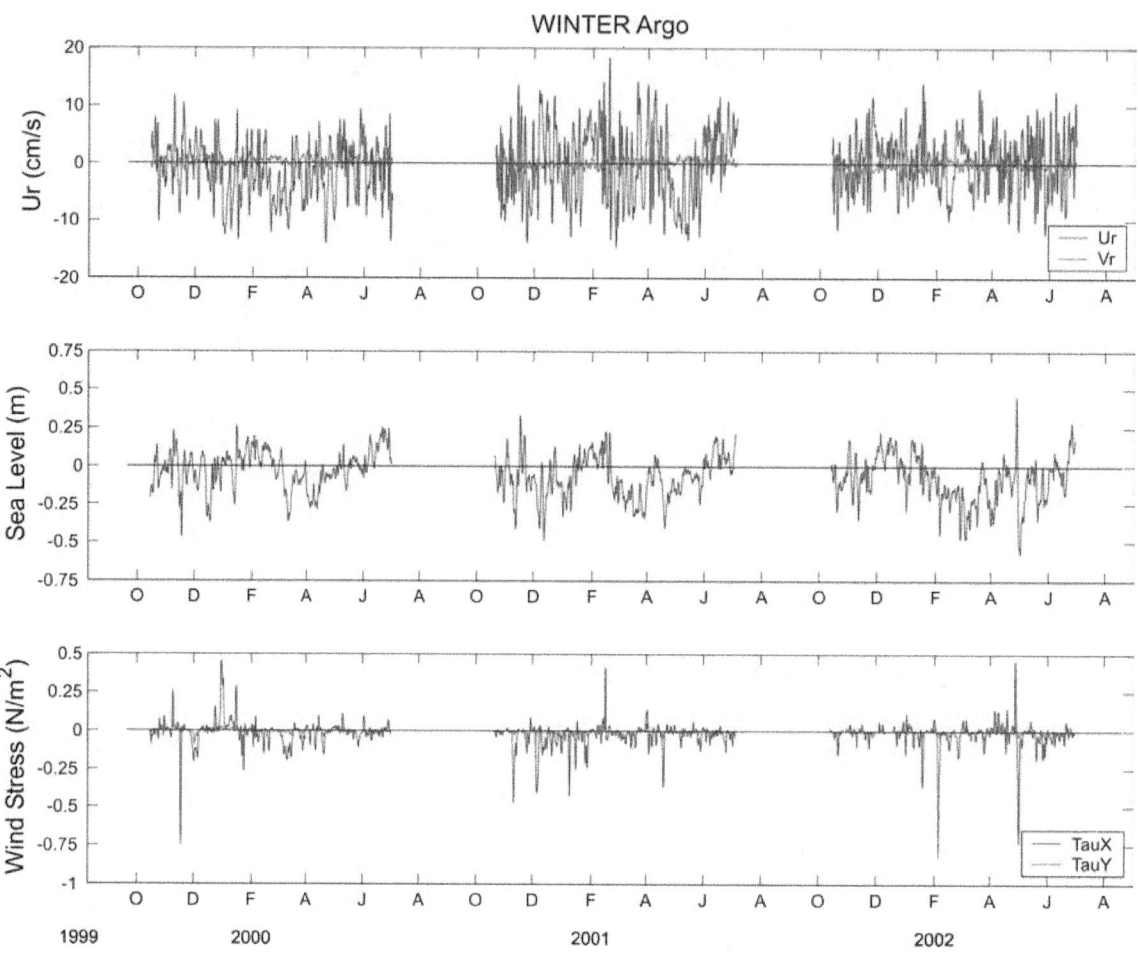

Figure 8. Time series of currents, demeaned sea level, and along- and cross-shore component of wind stress at ARGO for all landfast ice periods.

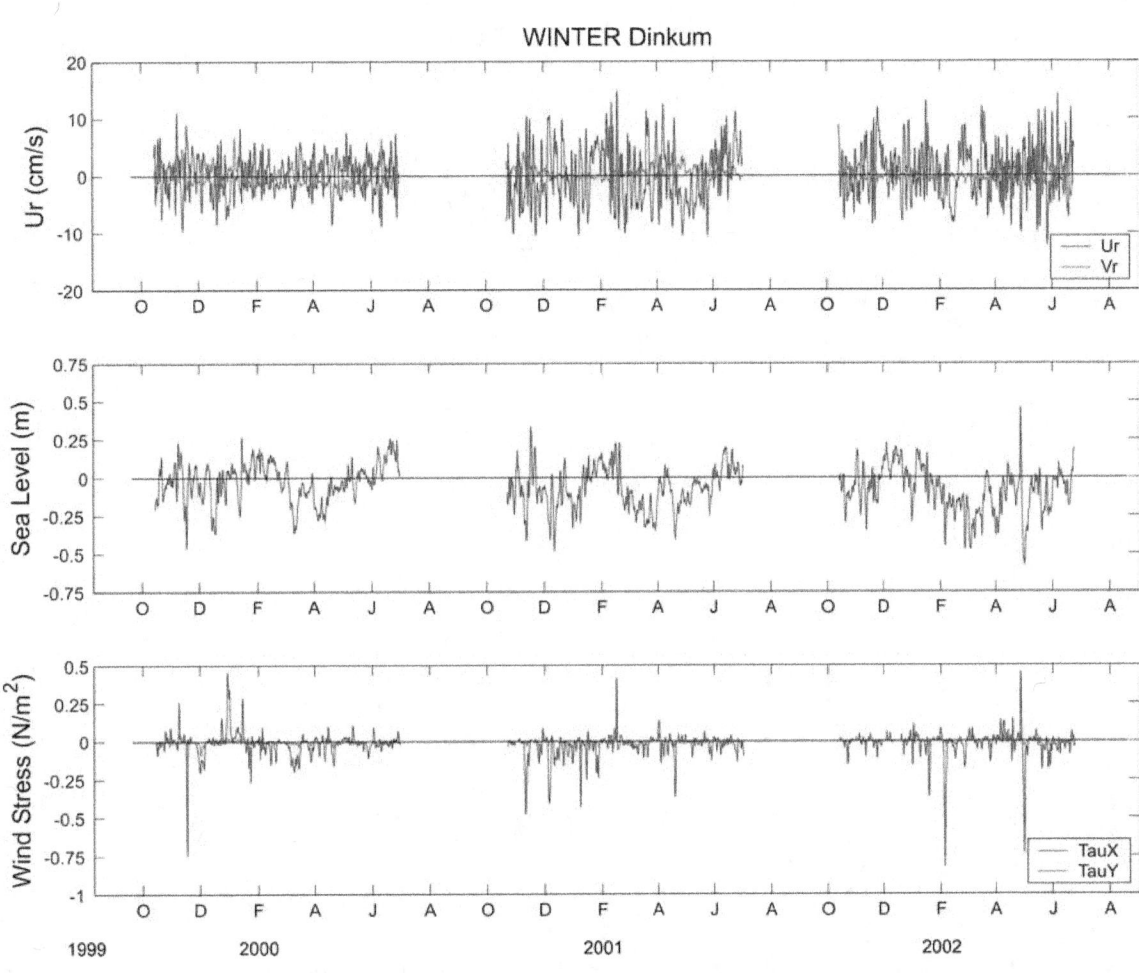

Figure 9. Time series of currents, demeaned sea level, and along- and cross-shore component of wind stress at DINKUM for all landfast ice periods.

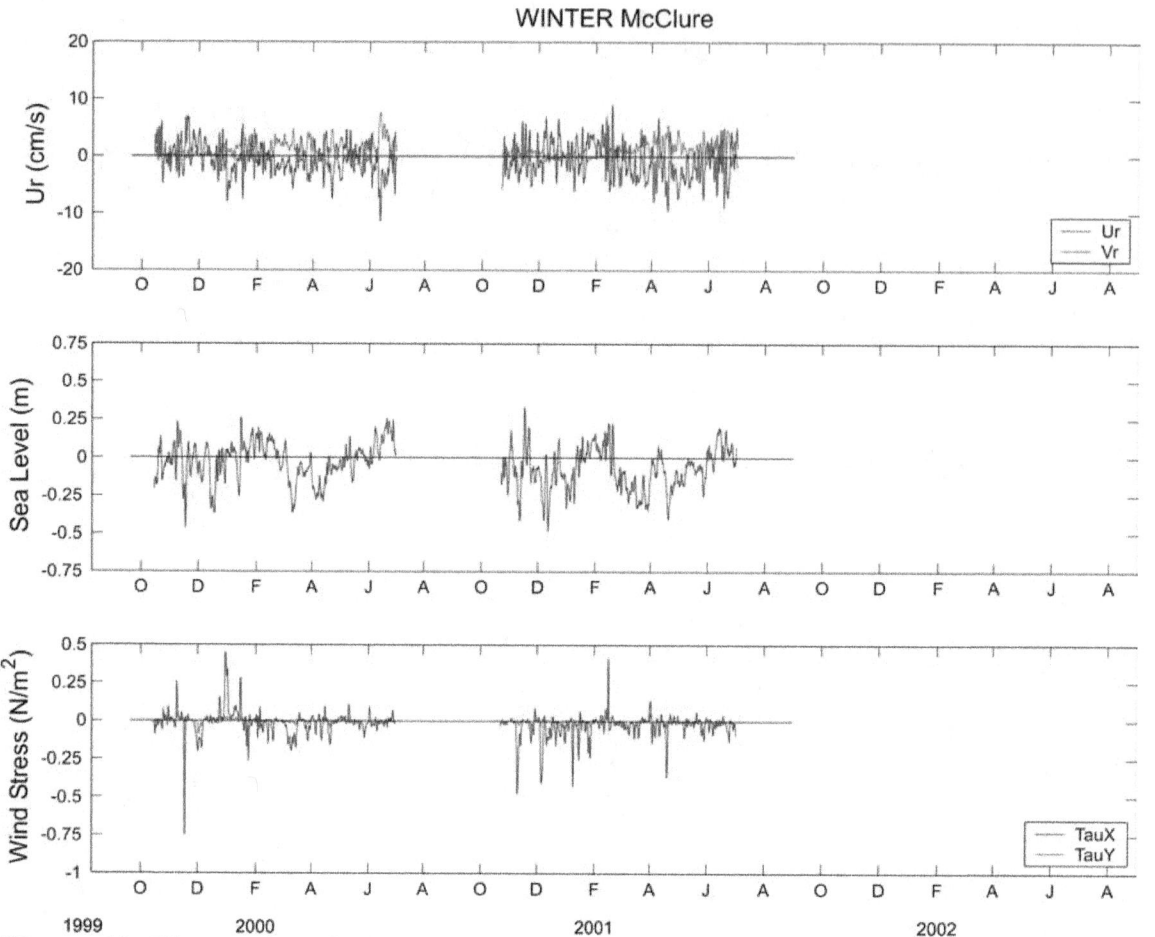

Figure 10. Time series of currents, demeaned sea level, and along- and cross-shore component of wind stress at McCLURE for the 1999-2000 and 2000 – 2001 landfast ice periods.

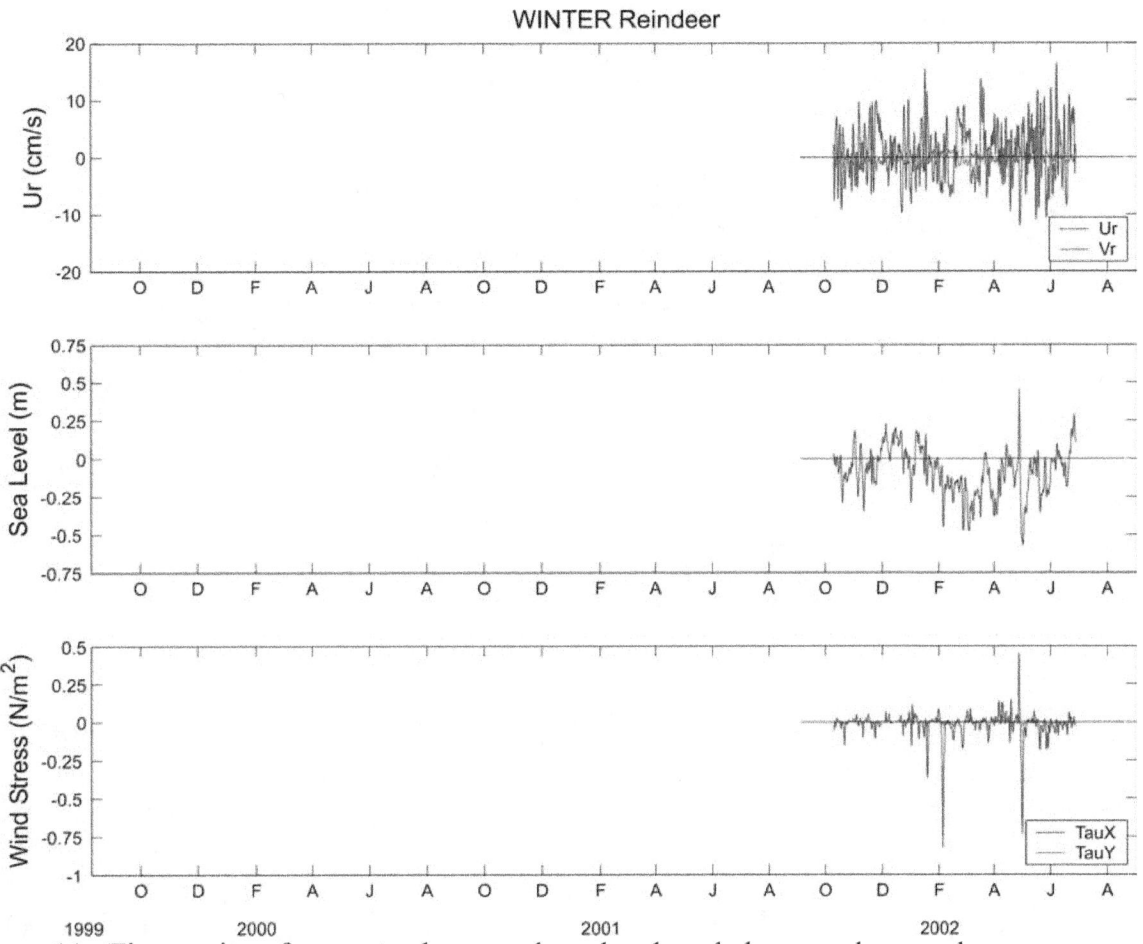

Figure 11. Time series of currents, demeaned sea level, and along- and cross-shore component of wind stress at REINDEER for the 2001 – 2002 landfast ice period

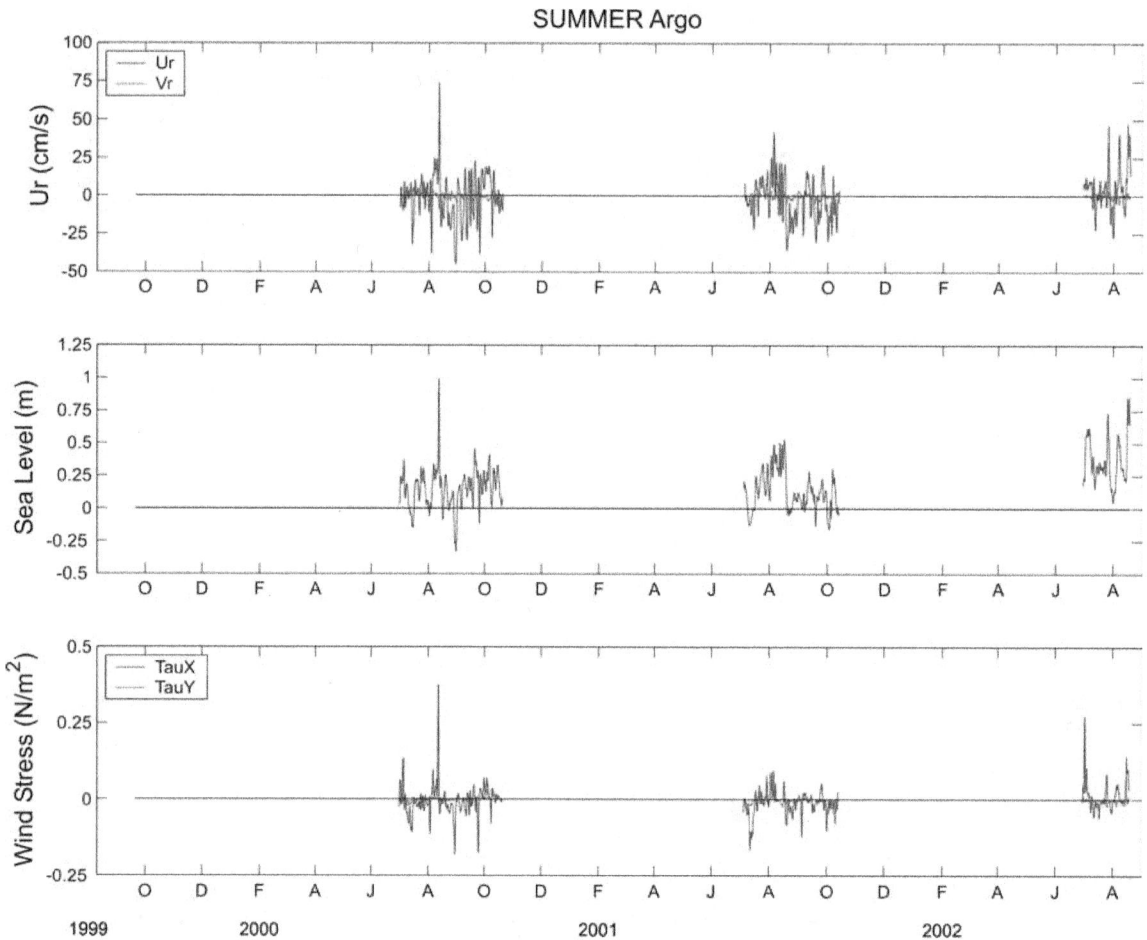

Figure 12. Time series of currents, demeaned sea level, and along- and cross-shore component of wind stress at ARGO for all open water periods.

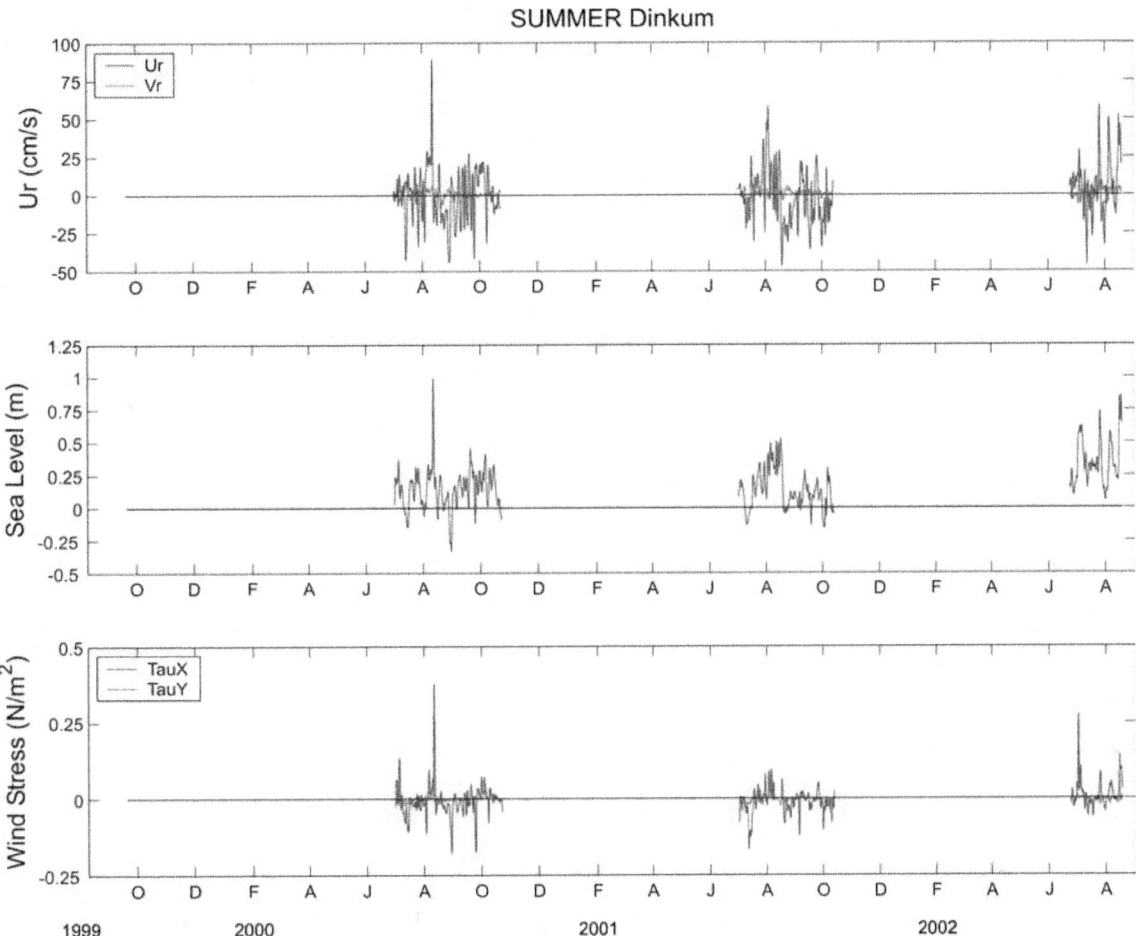

Figure 13. Time series of currents, demeaned sea level, and along- and cross-shore component of wind stress at DINKUM for all open water periods.

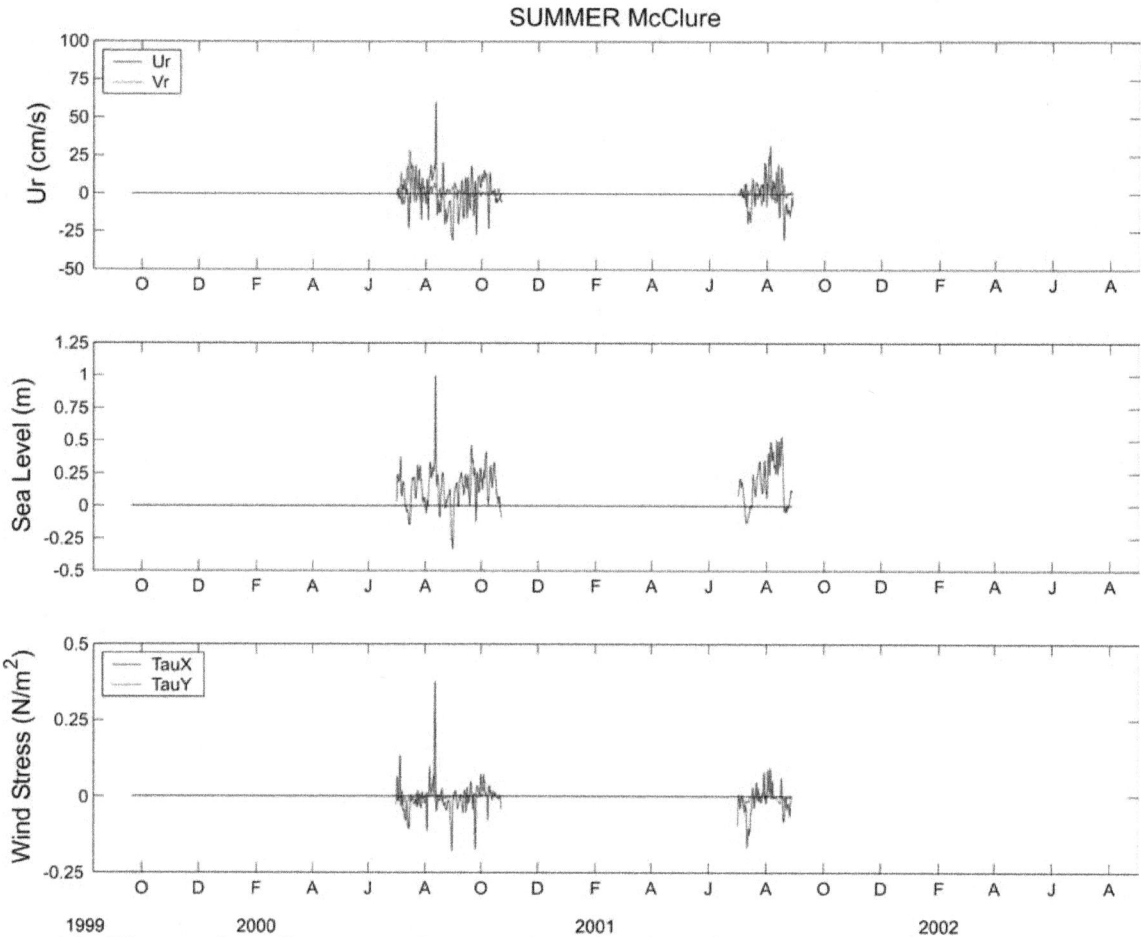

Figure 14. Time series of currents, demeaned sea level, and along- and cross-shore component of wind stress at MCCLURE for the open water periods of 2000 and 2001.

30

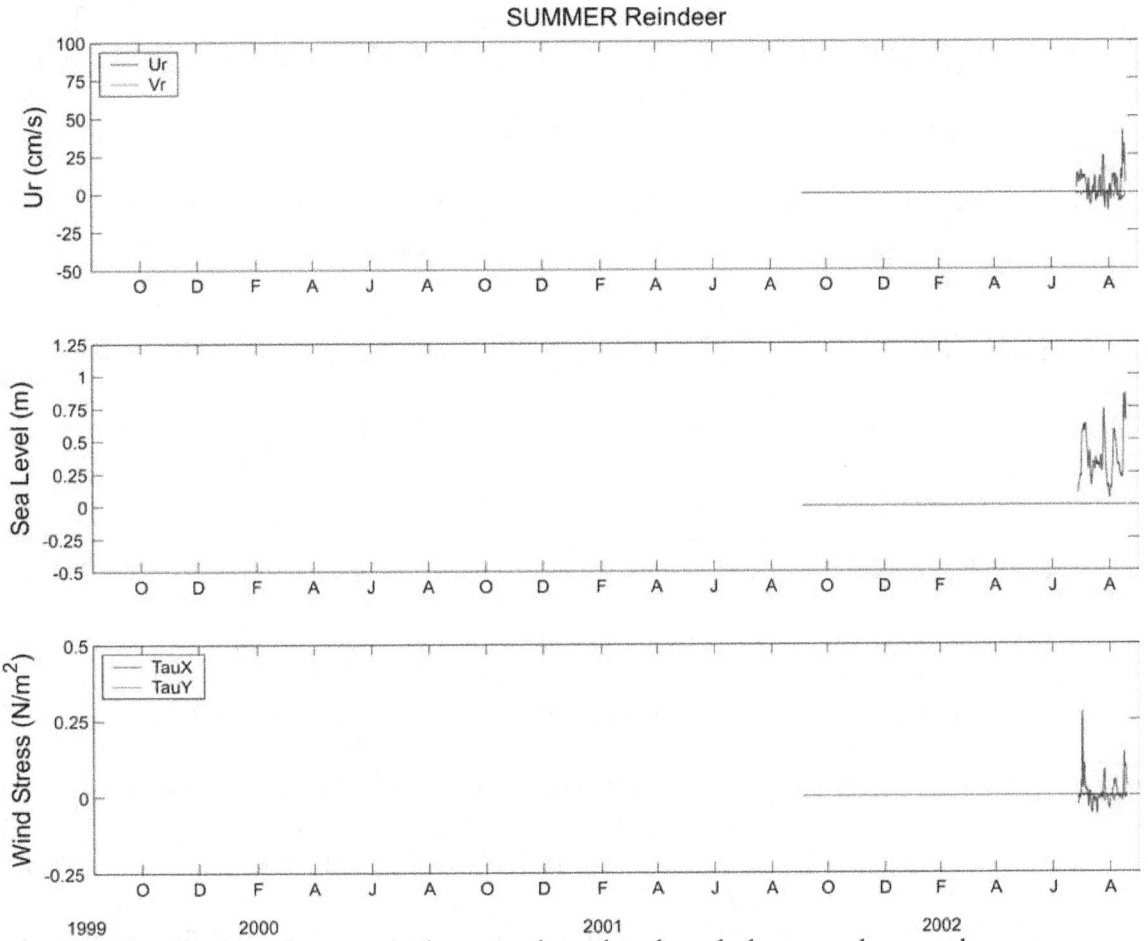

Figure 15. Time series of currents, demeaned sea level, and along- and cross-shore component of wind stress at REINDEER for the open water period of 2002.

Summary statistics for the currents and winds for each year and season are listed in **Tables 6 – 8** as a function of record length and season (landfast versus open water) as defined by the ADCP parameters. The current meter data were filtered prior to computing the statistics in order to focus on the subtidal properties of the flow field. The tidal properties are discussed separately later. Statistical significance is based on 95% confidence limits (listed in the tables) using the effective number of degrees of freedom (N_{eff}), computed as $N_{eff} = N\Delta t/\tau$. Here Δt is the sampling interval, N is the number of data points in the time series, and τ is the integral time scale of the currents or winds. The integral time scale is the decay time scale for a current or wind event and is the time required to obtain a new independent observation in an auto-correlated time series.

The winds are weakly westward with record-length averages ranging from $1 - 3$ m s^{-1} (depending upon deployment period) and statistically different from zero at the 95% confidence level. However, mean westward winds do not prevail throughout the year. For example, the mean wind was westward during the open water period of 1999-2000, but not significantly different from zero during the landfast ice period of that deployment. The opposite situation occurred in 2000-2001 and 2001-2002, when mean winds were westward during the landfast ice period, but not significantly different from zero during the open water seasons of these two years. The open water seasonal mean along-shelf wind, averaged over all years, is ~1m-s^{-1} and thus substantially smaller than the ~3.5 m-s^{-1} mean wind speed indicated for summer along the Beaufort coast in the climatology of *Brower et al.* [1988]. There is also very little difference in the wind variances among the deployment years and between seasons. The lack of a distinct annual cycle in Deadhorse winds contrasts with the prominent annual cycle in winds computed over the southern Canada Basin using synoptic forecast fields [*Furey*, 1998]. He found that the winds are westward on average from fall through spring, while in summer they are weakly eastward. He found a distinct annual cycle in wind variance, especially in the zonal velocity component, with the variance being three times greater in winter than in summer. Although the data sets and time periods used in comparing these annual cycles differ, this discussion suggests that there might be a cross-shelf gradient in wind stress. Mesoscale effects could be responsible for cross-shelf shears in the wind field. For example, sea-breezes (open water season only) promote westward coastal winds with this influence limited to the innermost 25 km of the shelf according to *Kozo's* [1982b] model results. In winter, the mountain barrier effect might influence winds at Deadhorse [*Kozo*, 1984] with this phenomenon occurring when atmospheric pressure systems force cold, polar air masses southward towards the Brooks Range. *Kozo* [1984] estimated that this baroclinic effect occurs up to 20% of the time during winter. However, his estimate was based on limited observations conducted during the 1970s. The frequency in which the mountain barrier baroclinic effect occurs should vary interannually in association with year-to-year differences in the large scale atmospheric pressure field over the arctic.

For most moorings and deployment periods the mean current vectors are not significantly different from zero, and when significant, they are small with mean alongshore velocities being <3 cm-s^{-1}. In fact, the largest mean values occurred during the open water period in 1999 when a statistically significant mean westward flow was observed at all sites except MCCLURE. The relatively large mean values for this portion of the record are biased, however, by the strong easterly storm event that occurred in early October 1999. Our mean values are somewhat surprising given the general belief that the mean flow is westward during the open water season [*Barnes and Reimnitz*, 1974; *Wiseman et al.*, 1974].

Table 6. Current and wind statistics 1999 – 2000. The direction toward which the mean velocity vector points is Θ_M. For the principal axis, % refers to the percentage of the velocity variance accounted for by the component projected onto the axis with orientation Θ_P. The mean north-south <V> and east-west <U> velocity components and $\pm$ the 95% confidence limits are listed. The latter are computed using N_{eff} based on the integral time scale (τ) determined from the first zero crossing of the autocorrelation function. Values significantly different from zero are italicized. The variances (s^2) of the V and U are given along with the ratio of the subtidal variance to the total variance, which is the variance of the filtered data divided by the variance of the unfiltered data.

Mooring	Mean Velocity		Principal Axis		Max Speed (cm s⁻¹)	τ (days)	<V> (cm s⁻¹)	s^2_V	<U> (cm s⁻¹)	s^2_U	$\dfrac{s^2_{subtidal}}{s^2_{total}}$
	Speed (cm s⁻¹)	Θ_M	%	Θ_P							
Full Record											
Argo	3.4	277	99	96	111	4.5	*0.4 ± 0.3*	4	*-3.4 ± 2.0*	172	0.87
Dinkum	2	307	98	119	110	4	*1 ± 1*	49	*-2 ± 1.4*	155	0.88
McClure	2.2	3	92	151	68	5.5	*2.2 ± 1.6*	87	*0.1 ± 1.0*	34	0.84
Winds (m s⁻¹)	1.3	250	90	77	25	3	*-0.5 ± 0.3*	6	*-1.3 ± 1.1*	36	-
Landfast Ice Period											
Argo	1.6	283	98	99	24	2.5	*0.4 ± 0.1*	1	*-1.6 ± 0.7*	23	0.71
Dinkum	0	-	94	141	20	2	*0 ± 0.3*	8	*0 ± 0.3*	54	0.54
McClure	1.1	29	89	176	14	3	*1 ± 0.6*	9	*0.6 ± 0.2*	1	0.43
Winds (m s⁻¹)	0.8	249	91	75	25	3.5	*-0.3 ± 0.4*	6	*-0.8 ± 1.3*	34	-
Open Water Period											
Argo	7.3	273	99	96	111	4.5	*0.4 ± 0.8*	5	*-7.3 ± 5.9*	205	0.90
Dinkum	6	306	99	117	110	4	*4 ± 1.4*	126	*-5 ± 3.0*	454	0.91
McClure	4.8	350	93	149	68	5.5	*4.7 ± 4.6*	244	*-0.8 ± 2.9*	102	0.88
Winds (m s⁻¹)	2.8	251	89	83	20	3	*-0.9 ± 0.4*	5	*-2.6 ± 2.1*	39	-

34

Table 7. Current and wind statistics 2000 - 2001.

Mooring	Mean Velocity		Principal Axis		Max Speed (cm s⁻¹)	τ (days)	$\langle V \rangle$ (cm s⁻¹)	s^2_V	$\langle U \rangle$ (cm s⁻¹)	s^2_U	$\dfrac{s^2_{subtidal}}{s^2_{total}}$
	Speed (cm s⁻¹)	Θ_M	%	Θ_P							
Full Record											
Argo	0.4	277	99	98	51	4	0.0 ± 0.2	3	-0.4 ± 1.4	89	0.83
Dinkum	0.5	50	98	120	58	4.5	0.3 ± 1	30	0.4 ± 1.0	85	0.83
McClure	0.8	11	81	136	60	4.5	0.8 ± 0.7	24	0.2 ± 0.8	23	0.71
Winds (m s⁻¹)	2.0	250	87	74	24	2.5	-0.7 ± 0.2	6	-1.9 ± 0.8	27	
Landfast Ice Period											
Argo	0.2	303	99	98	22	3	0.1 ± 0.3	2	-0.2 ± 1.4	42	0.81
Dinkum	0.5	47	98	125	15	5	0.3 ± 1	10	0.3 ± 1.0	19	0.74
McClure	1.0	4	94	154	11	4	1.0 ± 0.8	9	0.1 ± 0.3	3	0.52
Winds (m s⁻¹)	-2.6	250	88	73	24	1	-0.9 ± 0.4	6	-2.5 ± 1.5	27	-
Open Water Period											
Argo	0.9	261	99	97	51	4	-0.1 ± 0.5	5	-0.9 ± 4.0	205	0.84
Dinkum	1	57	98	119	58	4.5	0.4 ± 1.5	78	0.6 ± 4.5	242	0.85
McClure	0.5	43	80	131	60	3.5	0.4 ± 1.9	60	0.4 ± 2.5	71	0.78
Winds (m s⁻¹)	0.9	249	84	76	17	2.5	-0.3 ± 0.6	6	-0.8 ± 1.3	24	-

Table 8. Current and wind statistics 2001 - 2002.

Mooring	Mean Velocity Speed (cm s⁻¹)	Principal Axis Θ$_M$	%	Θ$_P$	Max Speed (cm s⁻¹)	τ (days)	<V> (cm s⁻¹)	s²$_V$	<U> (cm s⁻¹)	s²$_U$	$\frac{s^2_{subtidal}}{s^2_{total}}$
Full Record											
Argo	0.4	115	98	101	71	2.5	-0.2 ± 0.2	4	0.4 ± 1.0	70	0.82
Dinkum	0.9	115	97	126	102	3	-0.4 ± 0.7	39	0.8 ± 1.0	70	0.82
Reindeer	1	120	96	104	79	3	*-0.7 ± 0.3*	4	*1.2 ± 0.7*	41	0.79
Winds (m s⁻¹)	0.8	245	85	73	25	1.5	-0.3 ± 0.3	7	-0.7 ± 0.6	26	-
Landfast Ice Period											
Argo	0.4	110	98	106	23	2.5	-0.1 ± 0.2	3	0.3 ± 0.6	22	0.71
Dinkum	0.7	136	97	132	14	2	*-0.5 ± 0.3*	10	*0.5 ± 0.4*	12	0.63
Reindeer	0.9	112	98	109	20	2	-0.3 ± 0.2	3	0.8 ± 0.5	22	0.77
Winds (m s⁻¹)	0.9	268	88	72	25	1.5	0.0 ± 0.4	7	*-0.9 ± 0.8*	29	-
Open Water Period											
Argo	0.6	124	99	100	71	2.5	-0.3 ± 0.6	9	0.5 ± 3.6	207	0.87
Dinkum	1.6	90	98	125	102	3	0.0 ± 2.5	113	1.6 ± 3.6	220	0.86
Reindeer	2.7	127	95	99	79	2.5	*-1.6 ± 0.6*	7	*2.2 ± 2.2*	95	0.78
Winds (m s⁻¹)	0.9	197	80	76	20	1.5	*-0.9 ± 0.4*	6	-0.3 ± 0.9	19	-

36

Although the mean currents are small or negligible, the variability is large. Most of the current variance is contained in the along-shore velocity component where >~90% of the current variability is associated with this principal axis. For each mooring these axes are oriented approximately along-shore (e.g., northwest to southeast). Similarly, the winds blow primarily along-shore such that >85% of the wind variance is aligned along the east-west axis. As suggested by the current time series in the lowest panels of **Figures 5-7**, the current velocity variance changes seasonally, with the variance during the landfast ice period being roughly an order of magnitude smaller than the variance of the open water season. Along-shore current variances do not change significantly throughout the landfast ice season. This contrasts with findings on the Chukchi Sea shelf [*Aagaard and Roach*, 1990; *Weingartner et al.*, 1998; accepted] where current variance is generally much higher from November through January than from February through April.

Figures 16 and 17 show the mean velocity profiles projected along the major and minor principal axis for the landfast ice period at Reindeer for all eastward and westward flow events. The depth axis is the scaled depth which varies from 0 for the bin closest to the ADCP transducer to 1 for the bin nearest to the ice. The scaling takes into account the changing depth of the water column due either to ice growth or sea level fluctuations. In both cases the mean velocity varies by ~1 cm s^{-1} over the depth of the water column. The open water season velocity profiles are considerably different under eastward and westward flows due to the stratifying influence of freshwater runoff. These profiles will be discussed in Section V.

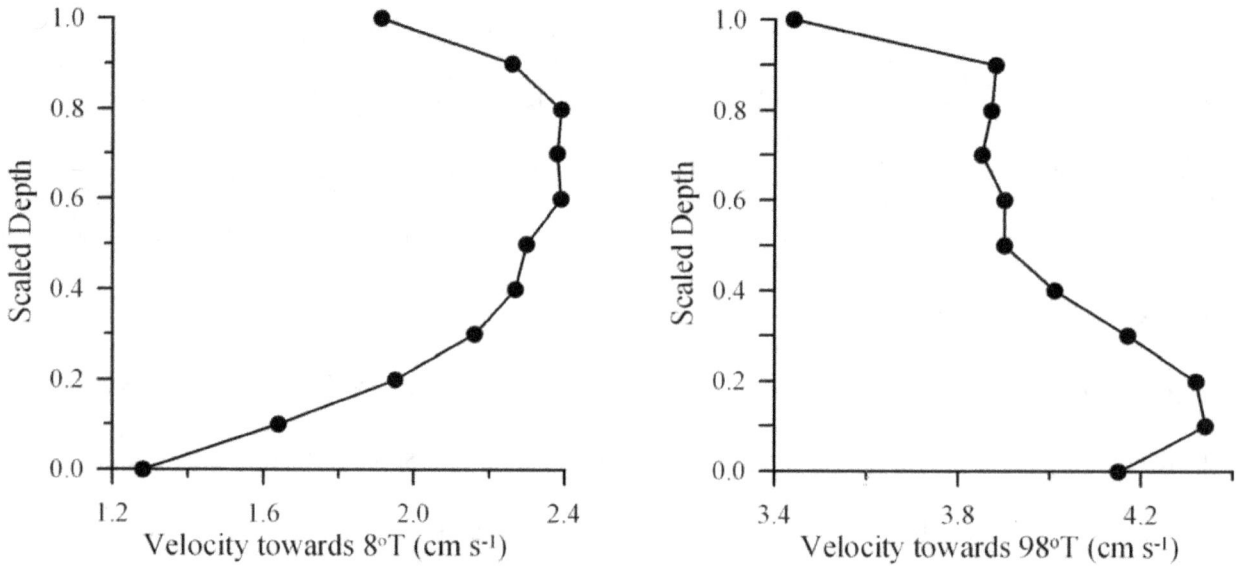

Figure 16. Mean velocity profiles for the cross-shore (left) and alongshore (right) velocity components during eastward flow conditions at REINDEER for the landfast ice season.

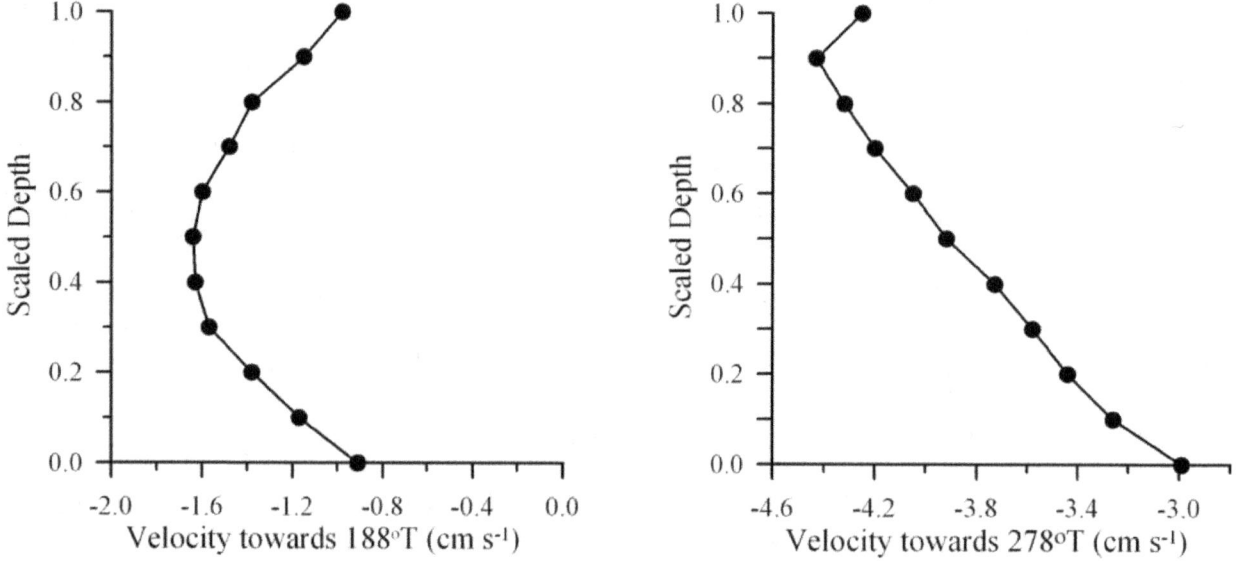

Figure 17. Mean velocity profiles for the cross-shore (left) and alongshore (right) velocity components during westward flow conditions at REINDEER for the landfast ice season.

These seasonal current speed differences are also reflected in the summary speed histograms constructed from the unfiltered data for all years (**Figure 18**). Less than 2% of all current speeds exceed 15 cm s[-1] during the landfast ice period, while more than 50% of the observations exceed this speed during the open water season. Our direct measurements during the landfast ice period are thus more in line with *Aagaard's* [1984] finding than with *Matthews'* [1981] inferences that current speeds could be as large as 35 cm s⁻¹. Speeds of this magnitude were never observed under the landfast ice except once at ARGO where the maximum speed was 25 cm-s⁻¹. In general we find that ~90% of the underice current speeds are ≤10 cm s⁻¹.

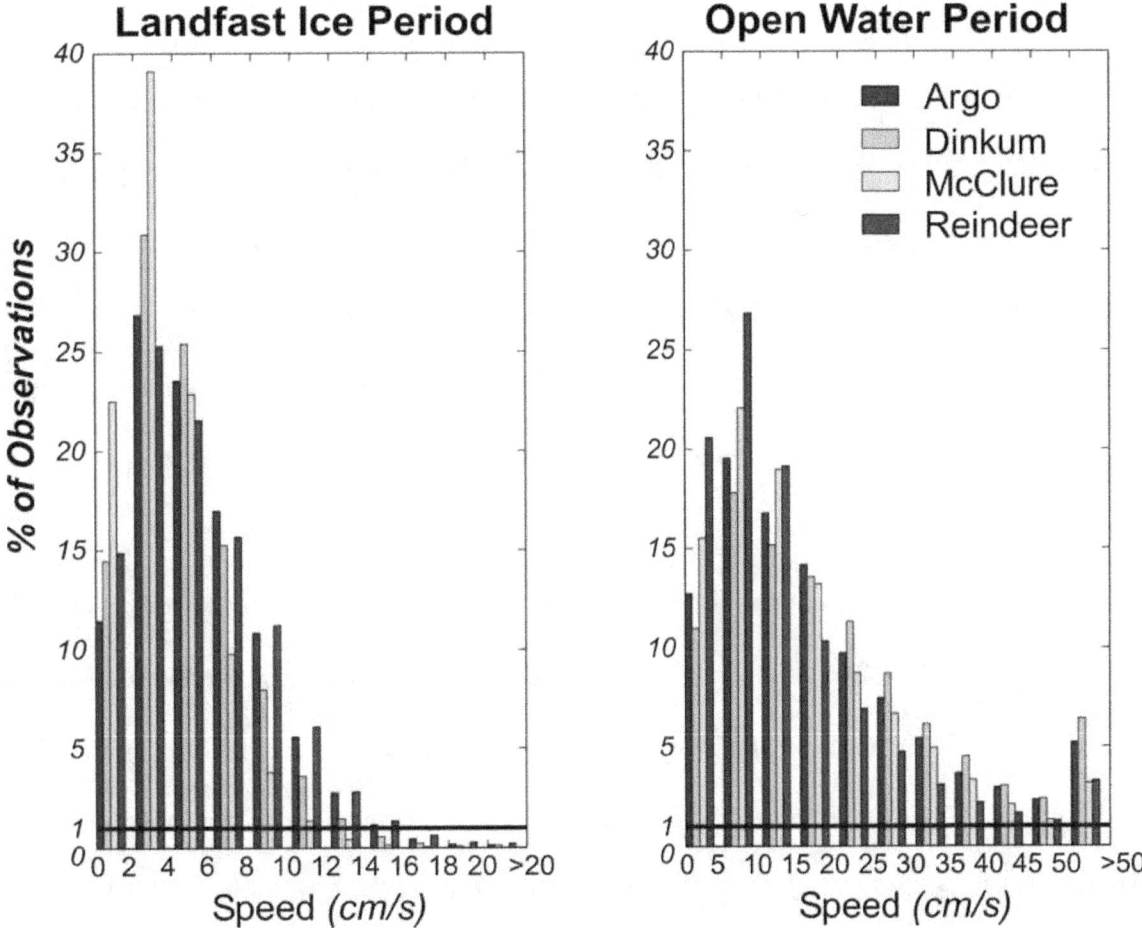

Figure 18. Histograms of unfiltered current speeds for the landfast ice and open water period at all moorings. The solid horizontal line indicates the 1% level.

The ratio of the subtidal to the total variance was calculated by comparing the variance from the filtered data to the unfiltered data. Subtidal variance accounts for from 50 – 80% of the total variance during the land fast ice period and for more than ~80% of the total variance during the open water period. There are differences in these ratios among years and sites, however. For example, the ratios at McCLURE are generally smaller than elsewhere, although not because of

39

smaller tidal current amplitudes, which as shown later, are similar at all locations. More likely these differences reflect the geometry of Stefansson Sound, which broadens from west to east. Current variations are consequently larger in the western and central portions of the sound (e.g., DINKUM, ARGO) than in the eastern sound (e.g., McCLURE). There are also interannual differences in this ratio. For example, at DINKUM the subtidal variance amounts to 54%, 74%, and 63% of the total variance for each landfast ice period. Interannual variations in these ratios reflect differences in the subtidal current variance and the differences between years are statistically significant at the 95% significance level based on the F-statistic. Although the subtidal variances differ significantly among years, there are no corresponding significant year-to-year differences in wind variances. This suggests little coupling between local winds and the underice currents, a point which we will return to later.

2. Tidal properties

The tides were estimated for each current meter record following *Foreman* [1978] and *Pawlowicz et al.* [2002]. The four largest constituents and periods (T_p) are the semi-diurnal, M_2, (lunar, T_{M2} = 12.42) and S_2 (solar T_{S2} = 12.00) and the diurnal O_1 (luni-solar, T_{O1} = 25.82 hrs) and K_1 (lunar, T_{K1} = 23.93 hrs). Tidal hodograph analyses are summarized in **Table 9. Figure 19** illustrates the various meaning of the terms that describe the hodograph. The M_2 constituent has the largest current amplitudes ($\sim$2 –3 cm s^{-1}), while the other species have amplitudes of $\leq$1 cm s^{-1}. The semi-diurnal tides execute nearly circular tidal motions and rotate anticyclonically, while the diurnal tides are nearly rectilinear (flattened ellipses) and oriented alongshore. Their rotational sense is ill-defined because the semi-minor axis is not significantly different from zero.

The semi-major axis, semi-minor axis, ellipse orientation, and Greenwich phase lag, calculated from successive 29-day overlapping segments of the current records at each mooring and for all years are shown in **Figures 20 – 35** for the four largest tidal constituents. Hodograph parameters vary throughout the year, particularly for the semi-diurnal species because of seasonal changes in ice thickness and extent, possibly larger-scale underice topography that affects frictional stresses between the propagating tidal wave and sea-ice, and stratification.

Although the seasonal variations are generally small, those associated with the spring freshet are substantial. Consider for example, the variation in the hodograph parameters of the M_2 tide at DINKUM (**Figure 24**). The semi-major axis varies seasonally and with depth but is a maximum of 5 cm s^{-1} in July 2001 beneath the ice during river breakup and a minimum of about 1.5 cm s^{-1} shortly thereafter near the bottom. Depth variations in tidal properties indicate either generation of an internal tide associated with stratification or vertical variations in eddy viscosity [*Danielson and Kowalik*, in press] associated with the strong pycnocline established as the spring

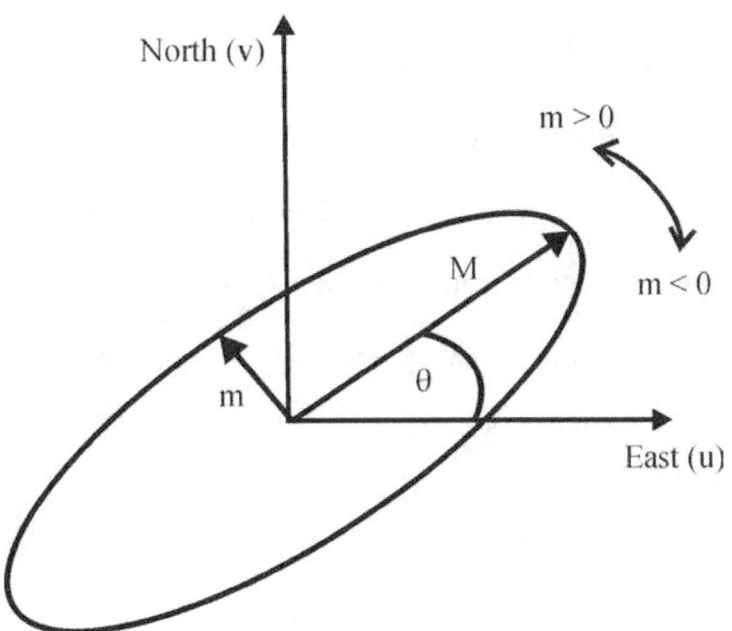

Figure 19. Illustration of the terms associated with the tidal ellipse (or hodograph) parameters: M, the semi-major axis, m, the semi-minor axis, and θ, the angle of inclination (from east). The tidal velocity vector rotates cyclonically (counterclockwise if m>0) and anticyclonically (clockwise) if m<0.

freshet flows beneath the landfast ice as discussed later. Tidal velocity shears are also small being ~0.003 s^{-1} at most and are not an important source of kinetic energy for mixing (as shown later). The tidal analyses suggest that hodograph properties vary seasonally throughout the landfast portions of all arctic shelves. While these variations are unlikely to be dynamically significant in the Alaskan Beaufort Sea, they might be important in the landfast ice zones of the Laptev and Kara seas, where tides are much more energetic [*Kowalik and Proshutinsky*, 1994]. Furthermore, the results suggest caution should be exercised when comparing tidal hodographs from short-term observations in the landfast ice zone with those from numerical tidal models. Differences between the two might not necessarily indicate model deficiencies but instead be due to seasonal variations in the tidal structure masked by short-duration measurements. We also note that the effect of landfast ice should have a strong influence on the structure of the super-inertial tidal (M_2 and S_2) currents. The boundary layers associated with these constituents might overlap in shallow water and promote mixing (assuming sufficient tidal energy dissipation). As the water depth increases the tidal boundary layers will separate, possibly allowing a stratified layer to be maintained in the middle of the water column. Conceivably this might lead to the development of a tidal front further offshore, but inshore of the landfast ice edge. Such fronts are capable of supporting an along-shore flow, and if present, likely to be found in the Laptev or Kara Sea where tidal velocities are substantially greater.

Table 9. Tidal ellipse parameters (based on the vertically averaged current component) for major tidal constituents at each site and year. Major (**M**) is the semi-major axis of the current ellipse and minor (**m**) is the semi-minor axis (negative values imply clockwise rotation of the velocity vectors and positive values imply counterclockwise rotation), The inclination (θ) is the angle **M** makes from the east. (The figure following the table illustrates the geometrical meaning of these terms.) The Greenwich phase lag is the time of the maximum constituent velocity relative to Greenwich. Values in parenthesis are the 95% confidence limits for each estimated parameter.

Name	Year	Major (M; cm s^{-1})	Minor (m; cm s^{-1})	Inclination, θ degrees from east	Greenwich Phase Lag
			Luni-solar diurnal K_1 (Period = 23.93 hours)		
Argo	1999	0.9 (0.2)	-0.1 (0.1)	7.1 (4.6)	273.2 (11.8)
Argo	2000	0.7 (0.2)	-0.1 (0.1)	0.6 (6.4)	271.6 (19.5)
Argo	2001	1.0 (0.3)	-0.1 (0.1)	173.8 (5.6)	83.6 (14.2)
Dinkum	1999	0.5 (0.1)	-0.1 (0.1)	19.6 (15.7)	239.3 (17.7)
Dinkum	2000	0.6 (0.2)	-0.2 (0.2)	170.1 (19.9)	79.5 (27.0)
Dinkum	2001	0.7 (0.2)	-0.3 (0.1)	170.1 (14.5)	83.3 (18.2)
McClure	1999	0.3 (0.1)	-0.1 (0.1)	57.2 (20.6)	238.0 (22.9)
McClure	2000	0.5 (0.1)	-0.1 (0.1)	80.7 (13.4)	254.6 (12.8)
Reindeer	2001	0.8 (0.2)	-0.0 (0.1)	162.1 (8.7)	101.4 (14.7)
			Principal lunar diurnal O_1 (Period = 25.82 hours)		
Argo	1999	1.1 (0.2)	-0.2 (0.1)	2.1 (4.4)	310.4 (10.6)
Argo	2000	1.0 (0.2)	0.1 (0.1)	179.6 (4.4)	121.8 (14.4)
Argo	2001	1.2 (0.2)	0.1 (0.1)	177.6 (4.2)	82.3 (10.6)
Dinkum	1999	0.5 (0.2)	-0.1 (0.1)	19.7 (16.5)	304.6 (20.5)
Dinkum	2000	0.8 (0.2)	0.1 (0.2)	170.8 (11.5)	99.9 (14.1)
Dinkum	2001	0.9 (0.2)	0.2 (0.1)	167.1 (11.1)	80.1 (12.3)
McClure	1999	0.4 (0.1)	0.0 (0.1)	49.4 (16.8)	297.7 (16.5)
McClure	2000	0.4 (0.1)	0.2 (0.1)	38.9 (24.5)	314.0 (22.8)
Reindeer	2001	1.0 (0.2)	0.0 (0.1)	163.2 (7.6)	80.5 (11.8)
			Principal lunar semi-diurnal M_2 (Period = 12.42 hours)		
Argo	1999	1.8 (0.1)	-1.3 (0.1)	28.4 (6.2)	62.4 (6.9)
Argo	2000	1.7 (0.1)	-1.3 (0.1)	27.0 (8.4)	81.5 (8.8)
Argo	2001	1.6 (0.1)	-1.3 (0.1)	35.4 (11.7)	55.0 (13.1)
Dinkum	1999	2.0 (0.1)	-0.6 (0.1)	93.0 (3.1)	18.5 (2.5)
Dinkum	2000	1.7 (0.1)	-1.2 (0.1)	78.0 (10.3)	34.8 (10.0)
Dinkum	2001	2.0 (0.1)	-1.0 (0.1)	81.6 (5.5)	17.8 (5.6)
McClure	1999	2.2 (0.1)	-0.2 (0.1)	78.9 (1.9)	28.5 (1.9)
McClure	2000	2.2 (0.2)	-0.4 (0.1)	94.8 (3.2)	53.4 (4.0)
Reindeer	2001	1.4 (0.1)	-0.8 (0.1)	139.4 (5.3)	321.1 (5.8)
			Principal solar semi-diurnal S_2 (Period = 12.00 hours)		
Argo	1999	0.8 (0.1)	-0.6 (0.1)	39.5 (17.7)	70.0 (17.1)
Argo	2000	1.0 (0.1)	-0.6 (0.1)	23.5 (10.8)	78.6 (10.6)
Argo	2001	0.8 (0.1)	-0.6 (0.1)	25.5 (16.6)	76.2 (16.0)
Dinkum	1999	0.9 (0.1)	-0.3 (0.1)	92.9 (7.0)	31.9 (6.6)
Dinkum	2000	0.8 (0.1)	-0.5 (0.1)	68.3 (18.9)	44.8 (18.0)
Dinkum	2001	0.8 (0.1)	-0.5 (0.1)	80.4 (16.7)	33.0 (16.3)
McClure	1999	1.0 (0.1)	-0.1 (0.1)	76.0 (4.0)	44.3 (4.7)
McClure	2000	1.0 (0.1)	-0.2 (0.1)	92.8 (6.8)	53.6 (10.7)
Reindeer	2001	0.7 (0.1)	-0.4 (0.1)	149.7 (10.6)	322.6 (11.1)

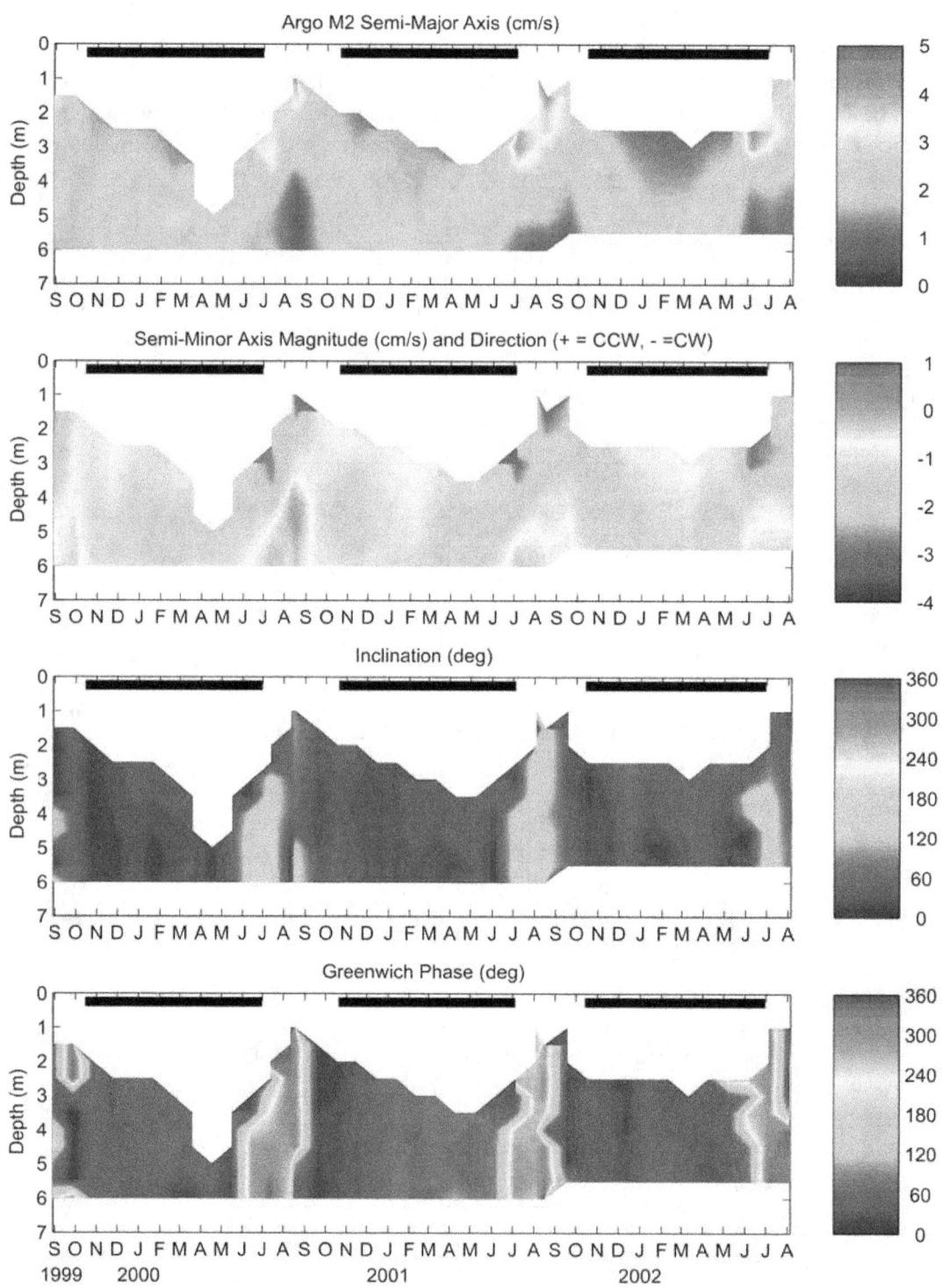

Figure 20. M₂ tidal properties at ARGO based on 29-day overlapping tidal analyses. The parameters are (from top to bottom) the major axis, minor axis, inclination, and phase. Solid black line indicates landfast ice season.

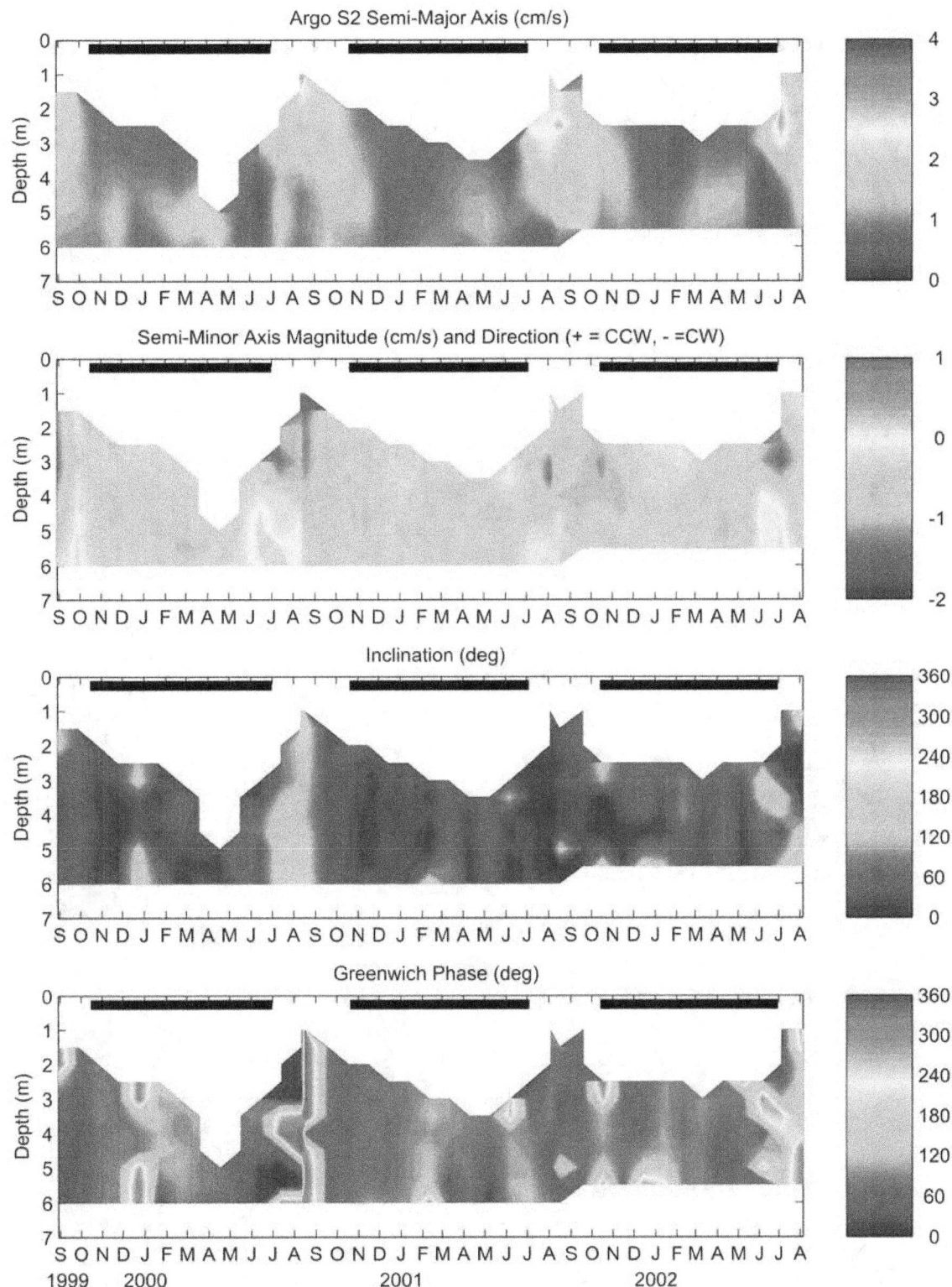

Figure 21. S$_2$ tidal properties at ARGO based on 29-day overlapping tidal analyses. The parameters are (from top to bottom) the major axis, minor axis, inclination, and phase. Solid black line indicates landfast ice season.

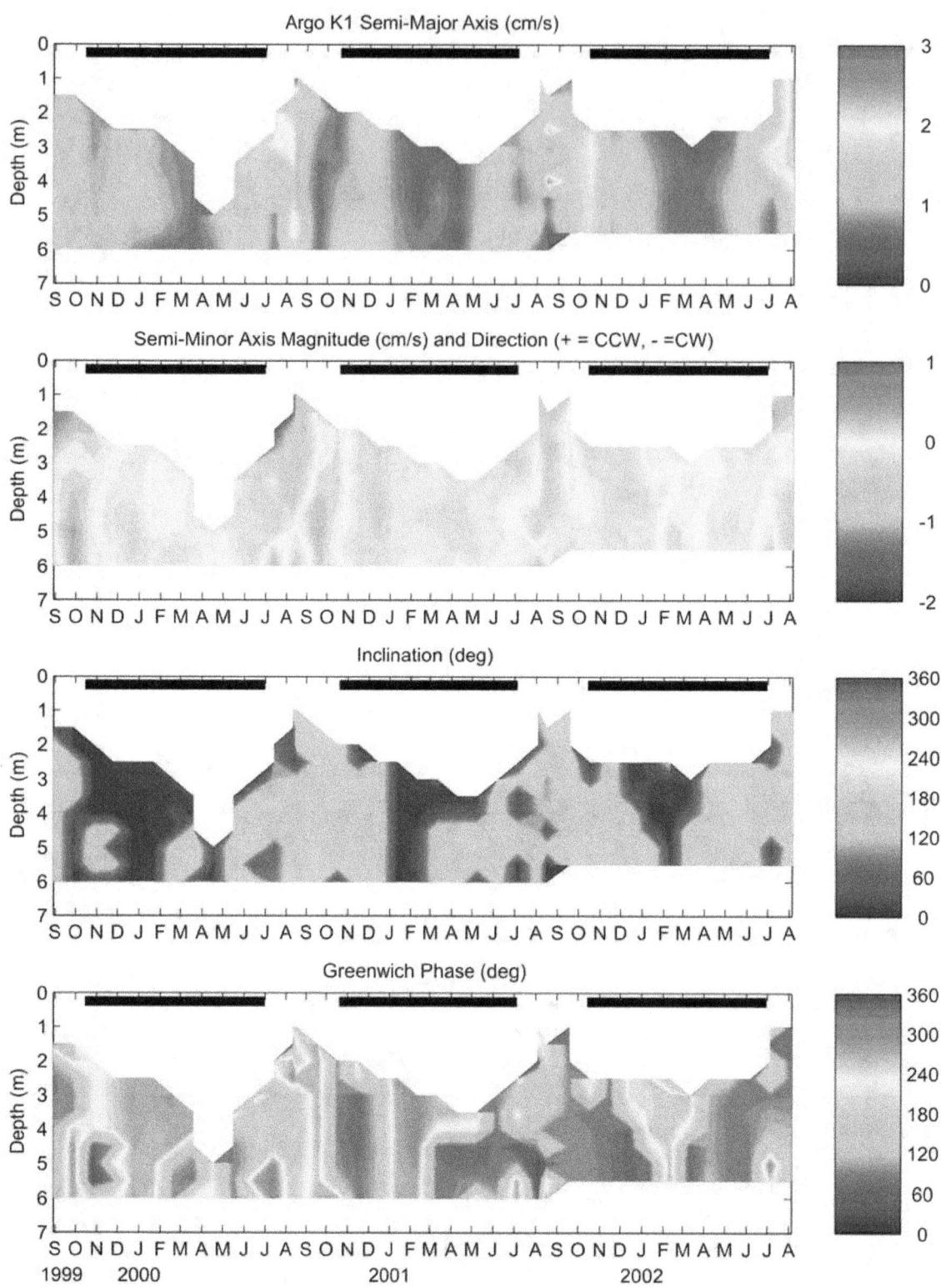

Figure 22. K_1 tidal properties at ARGO based on 29-day overlapping tidal analyses. The parameters are (from top to bottom) the major axis, minor axis, inclination, and phase. Solid black line indicates landfast ice season.

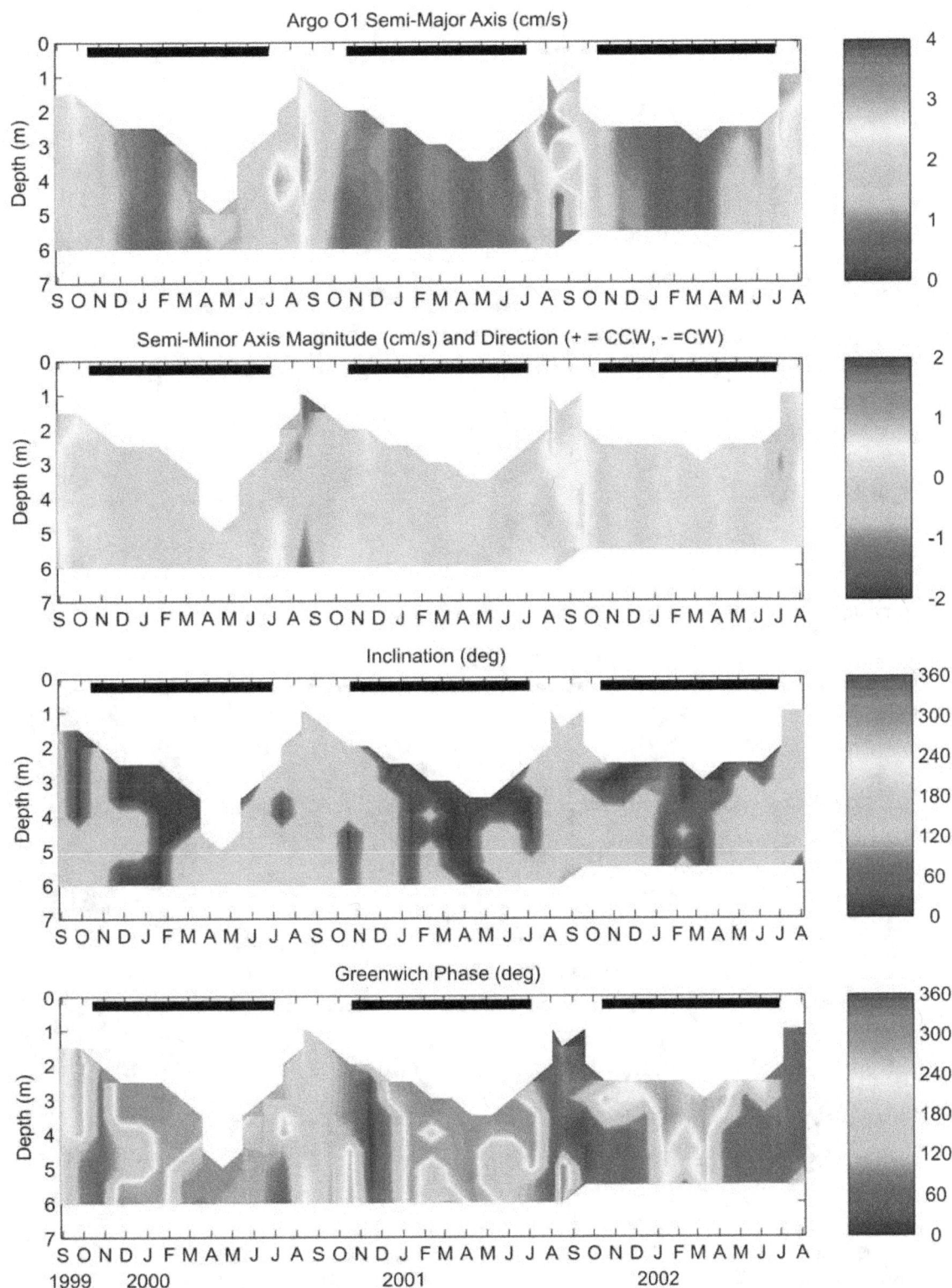

Figure 2 O_1 tidal properties at ARGO based on 29-day overlapping tidal analyses. The parameters are (from top to bottom) the major axis, minor axis, inclination, and phase. Solid black line indicates landfast ice season.

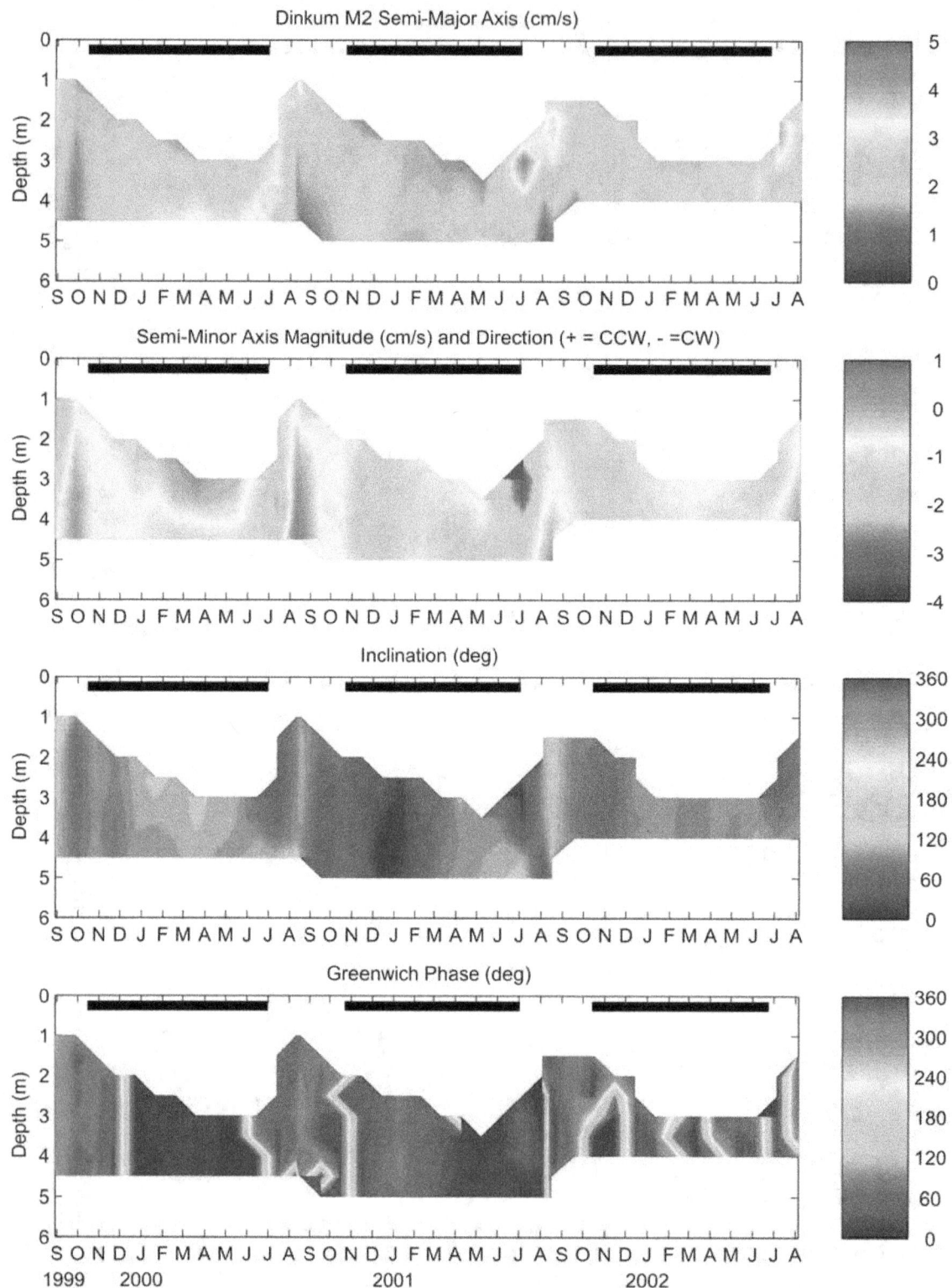

Figure 2 M$_2$ tidal properties at DINKUM based on 29-day overlapping tidal analyses. The parameters are (from top to bottom) the major axis, minor axis, inclination, and phase. Solid black line indicates landfast ice season.

48

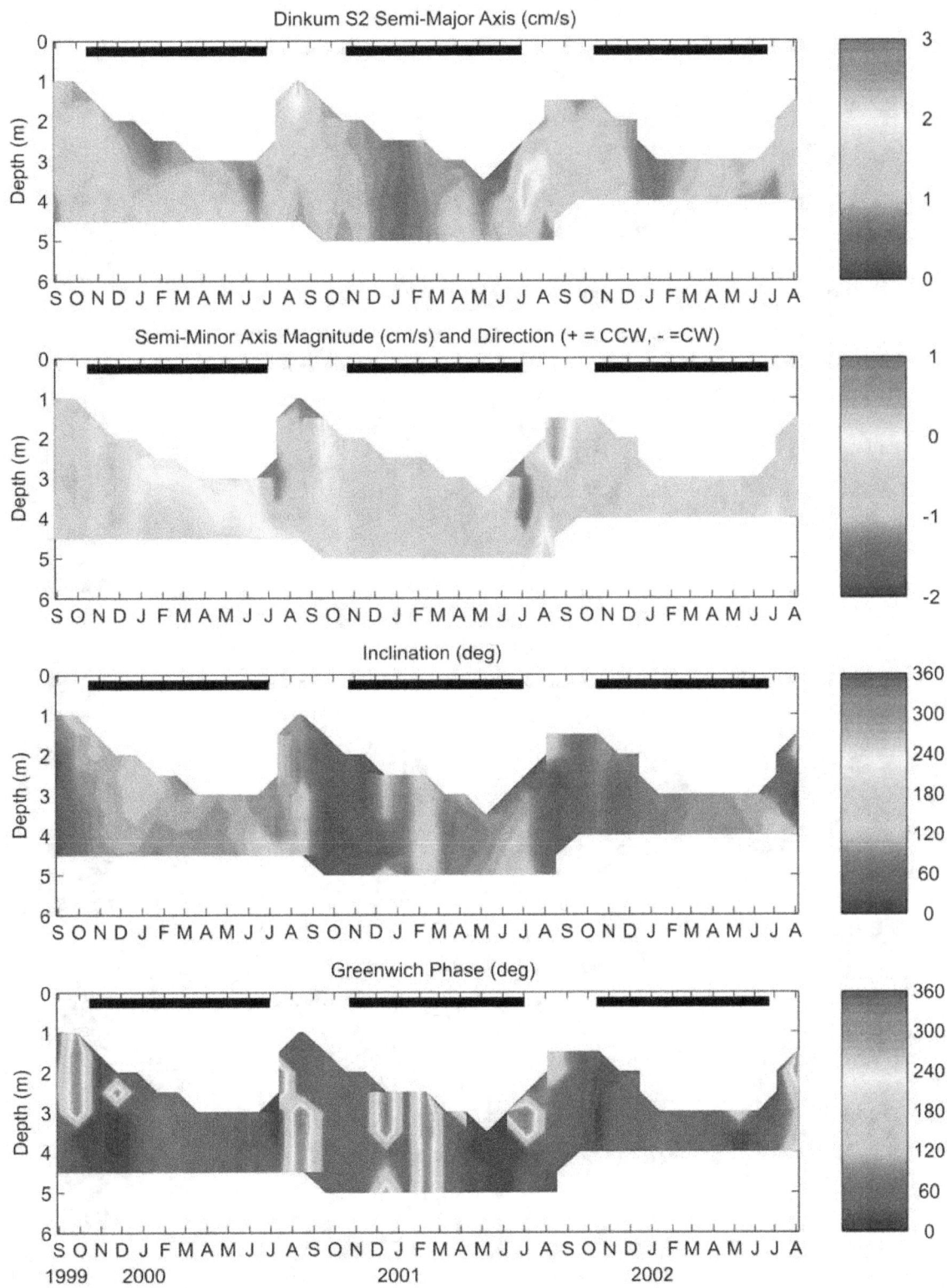

Figure 2 S_2 tidal properties at DINKUM based on 29-day overlapping tidal analyses. The parameters are (from top to bottom) the major axis, minor axis, inclination, and phase. Solid black line indicates landfast ice season.

49

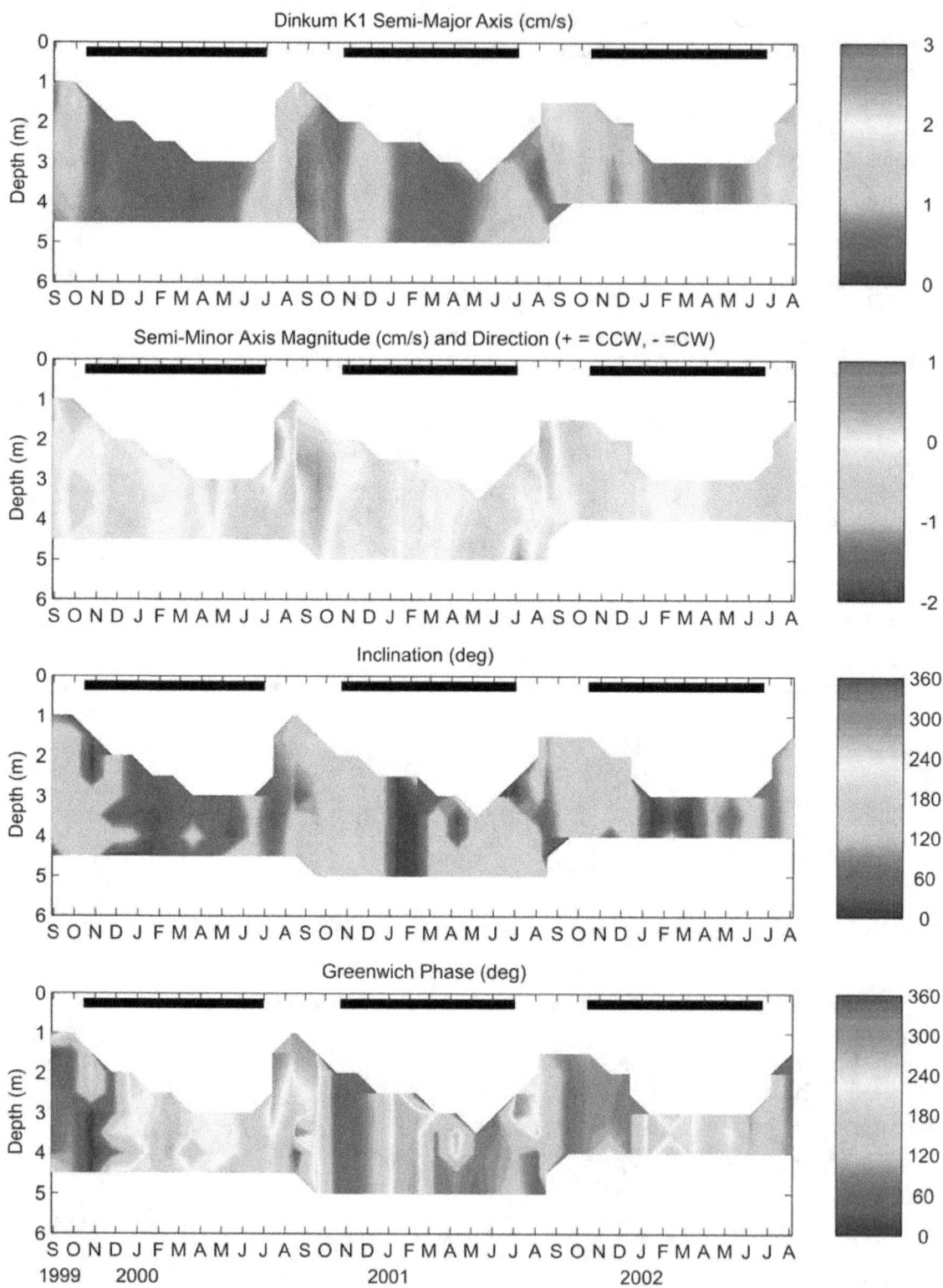

Figure 2 K$_1$ tidal properties at DINKUM based on 29-day overlapping tidal analyses. The parameters are (from top to bottom) the major axis, minor axis, inclination, and phase. Solid black line indicates landfast ice season.

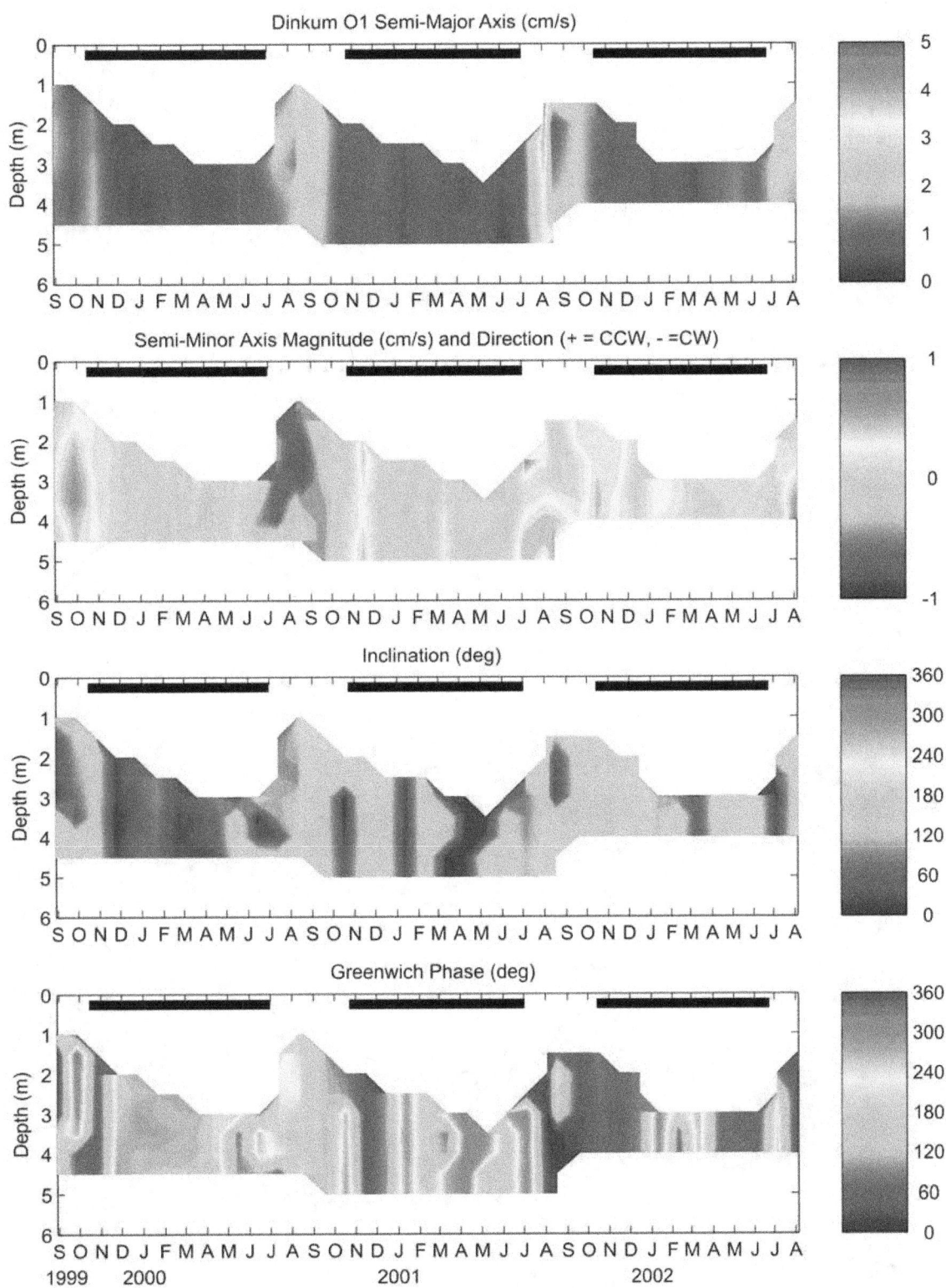

Figure 2 O_1 tidal properties at DINKUM based on 29-day overlapping tidal analyses. The parameters are (from top to bottom) the major axis, minor axis, inclination, and phase. Solid black line indicates landfast ice season.

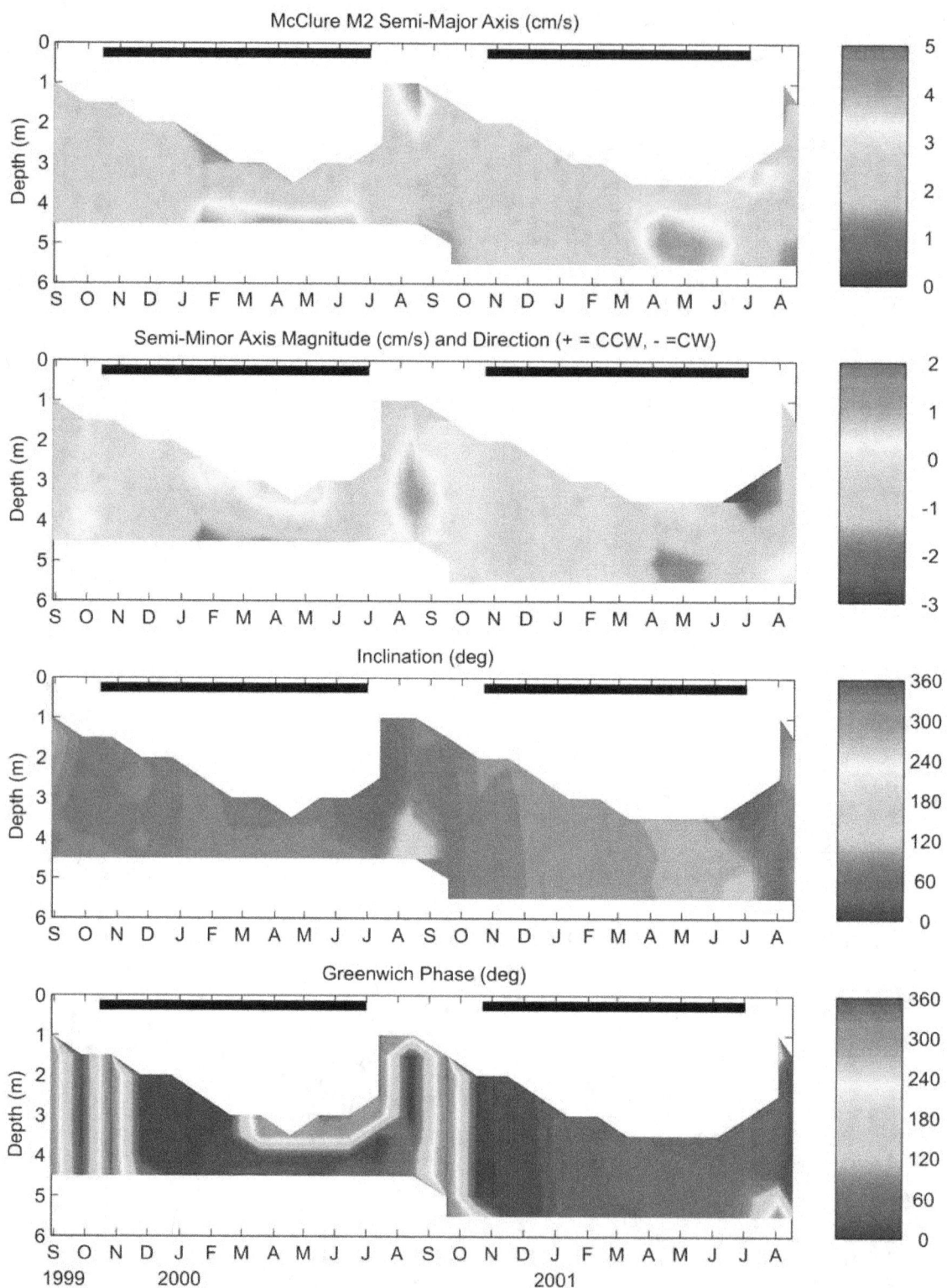

Figure 2 M$_2$ tidal properties at MCCLURE based on 29-day overlapping tidal analyses. The parameters are (from top to bottom) the major axis, minor axis, inclination, and phase. Solid black line indicates landfast ice season.

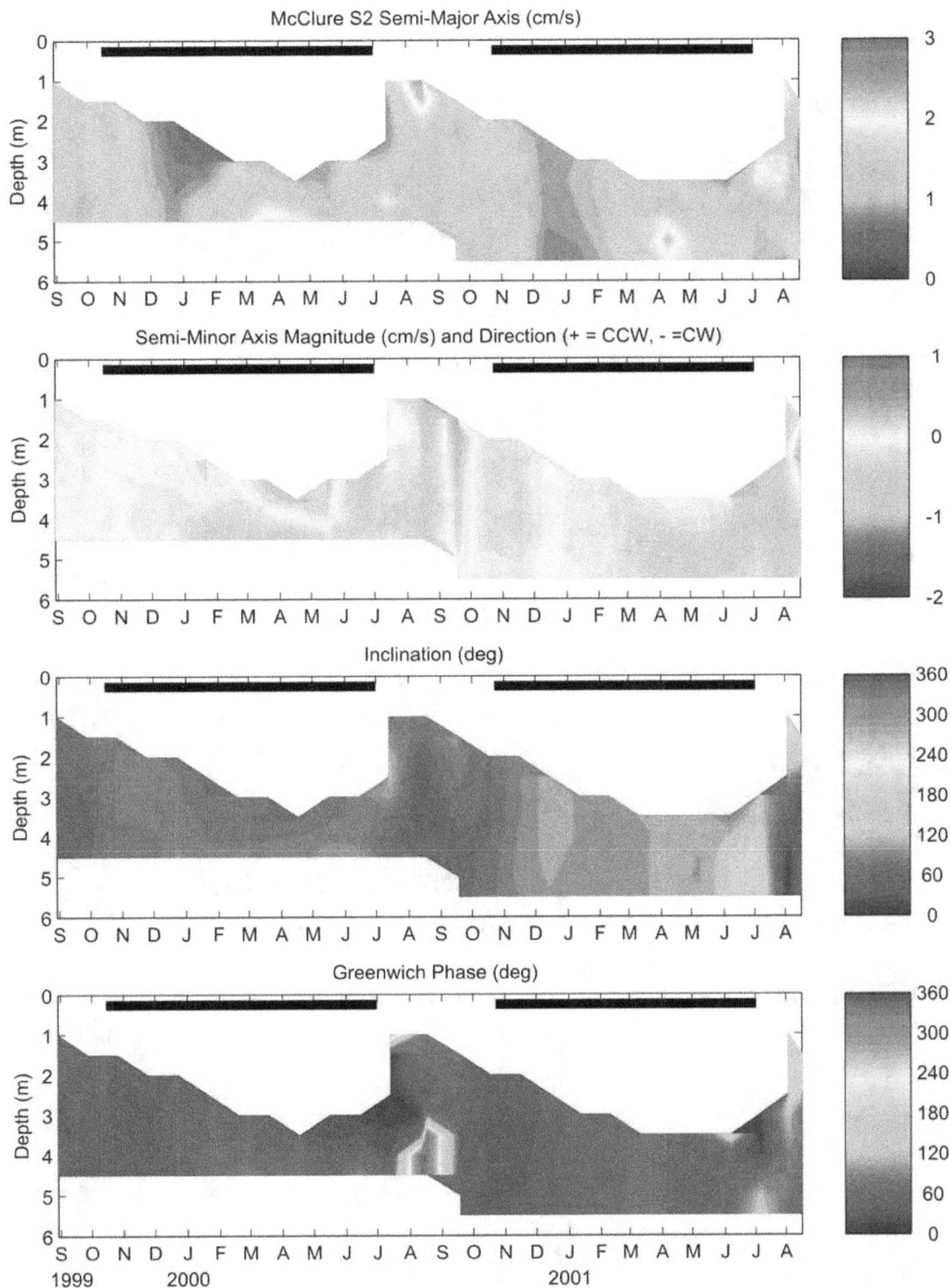

Figure 2 S_2 tidal properties at MCCLURE based on 29-day overlapping tidal analyses. The parameters are (from top to bottom) the major axis, minor axis, inclination, and phase. Solid black line indicates landfast ice season.

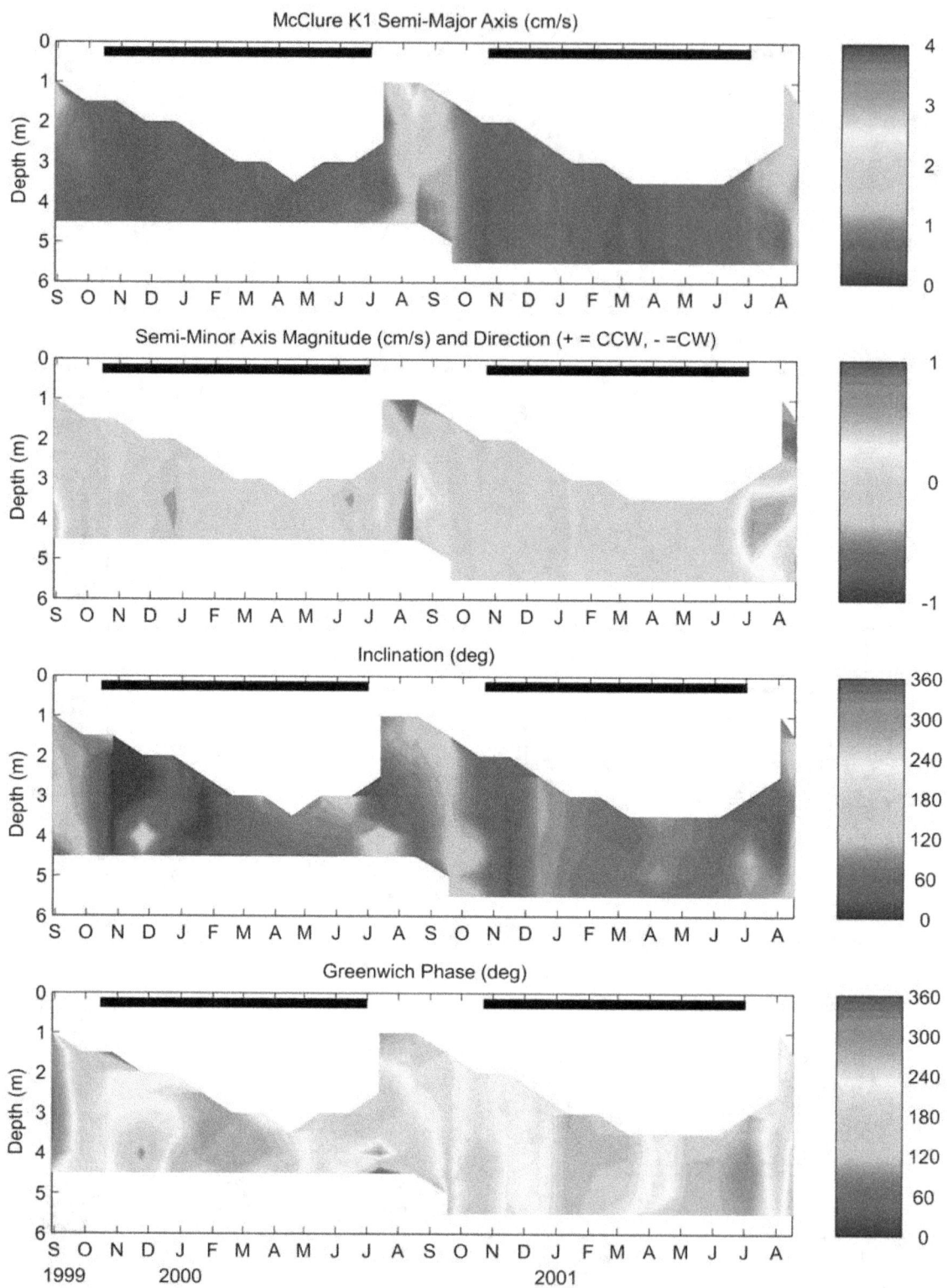

Figure ⬜ K$_1$ tidal properties at MCCLURE based on 29-day overlapping tidal analyses. The parameters are (from top to bottom) the major axis, minor axis, inclination, and phase. Solid black line indicates landfast ice season.

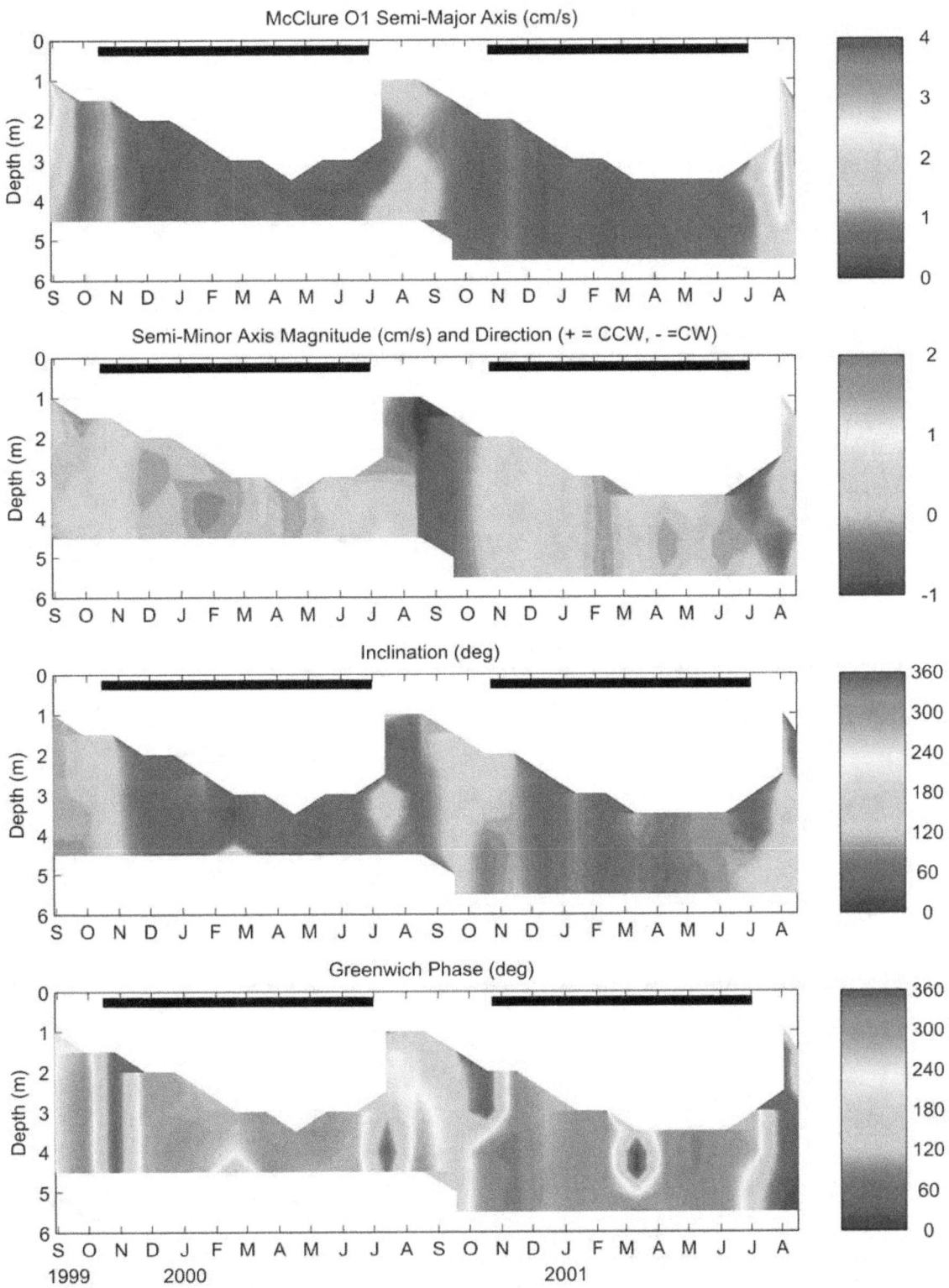

Figure ☐☐ O_1 tidal properties at MCCLURE based on 29-day overlapping tidal analyses. The parameters are (from top to bottom) the major axis, minor axis, inclination, and phase. Solid black line indicates landfast ice season.

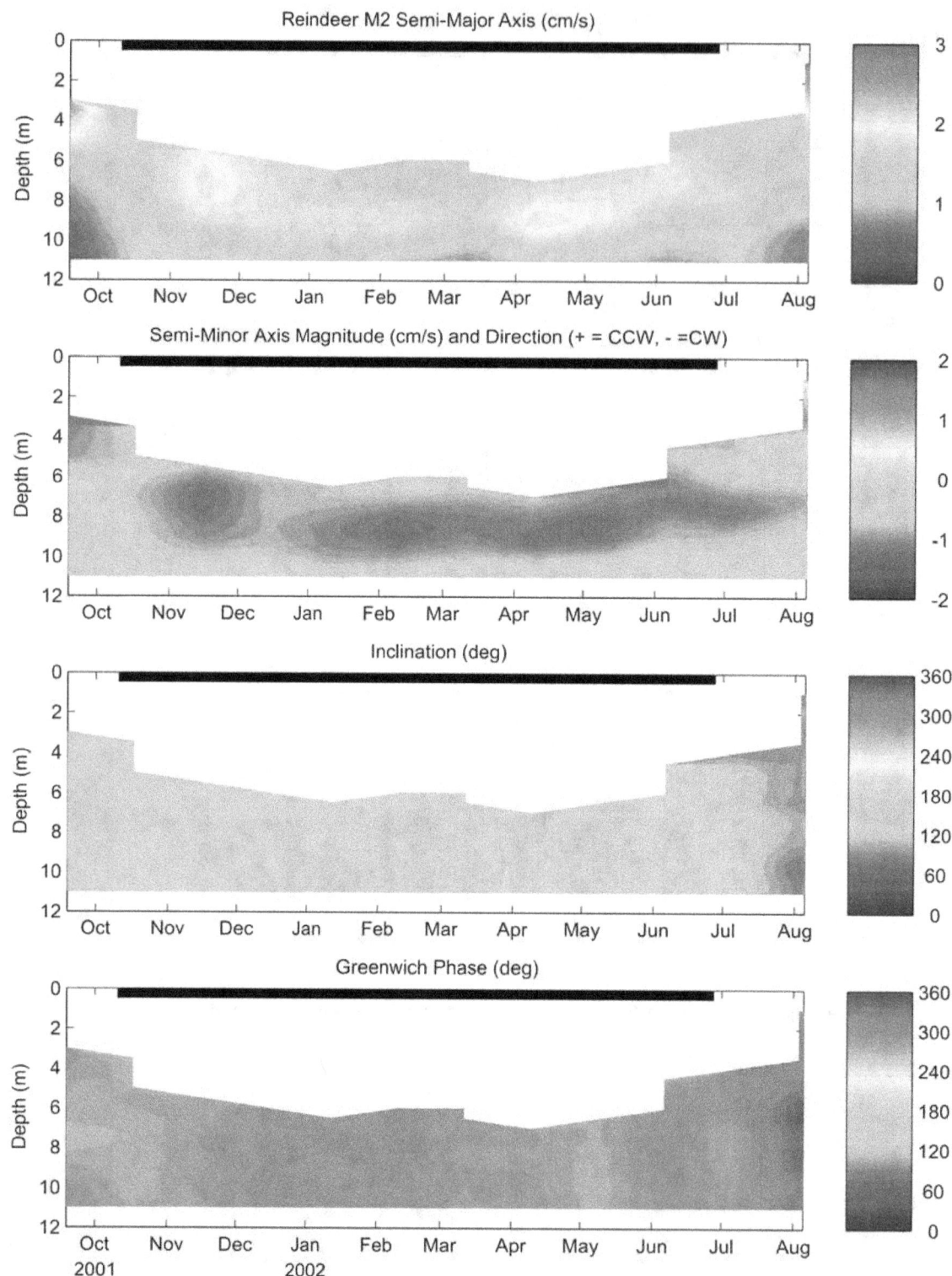

Figure □2. M₂ tidal properties at REINDEER based on 29-day overlapping tidal analyses. The parameters are (from top to bottom) the major axis, minor axis, inclination, and phase. Solid black line indicates landfast ice season.

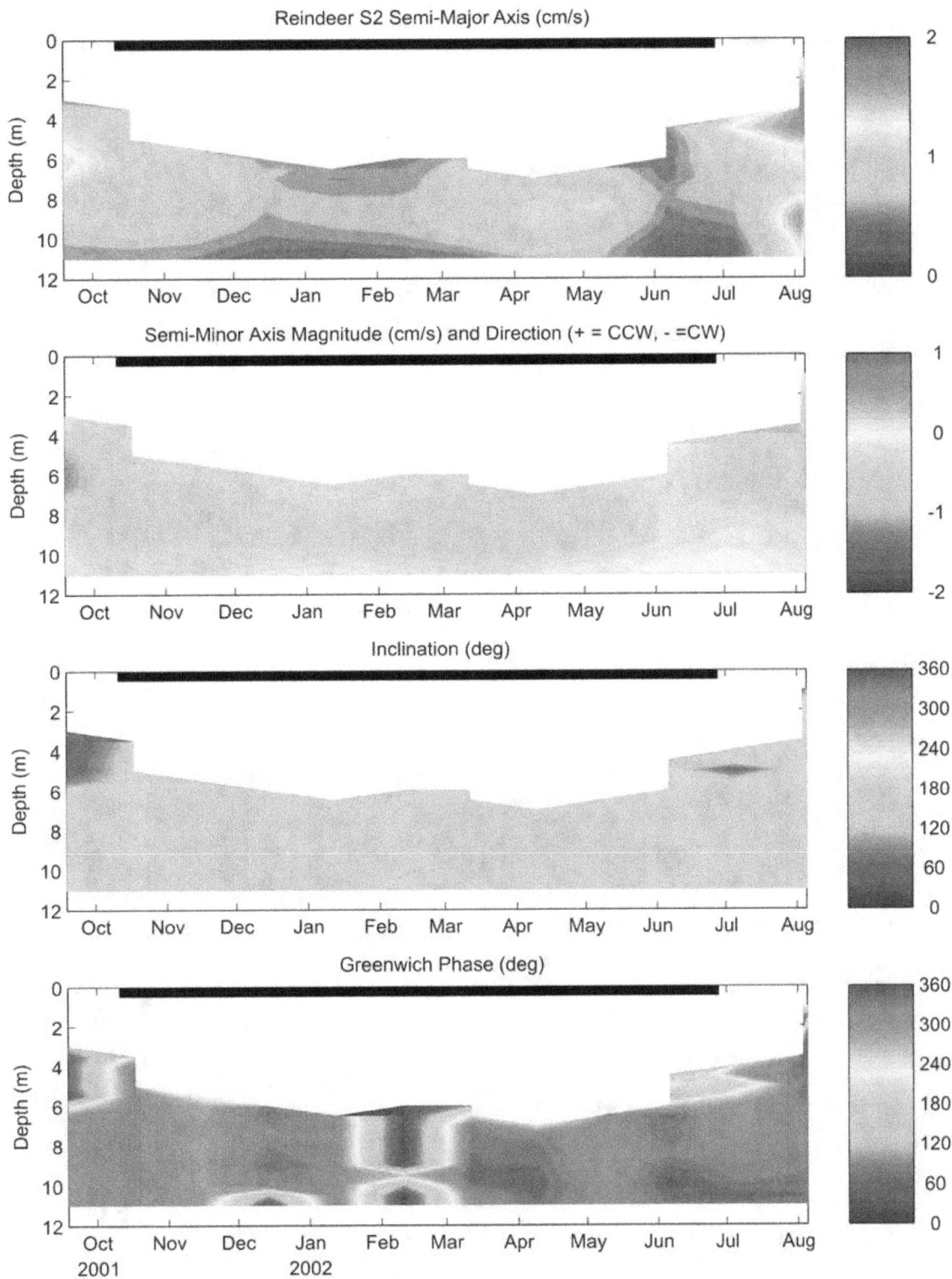

Figure □□ S₂ tidal properties at REINDEER based on 29-day overlapping tidal analyses. The parameters are (from top to bottom) the major axis, minor axis, inclination, and phase. Solid black line indicates landfast ice season.

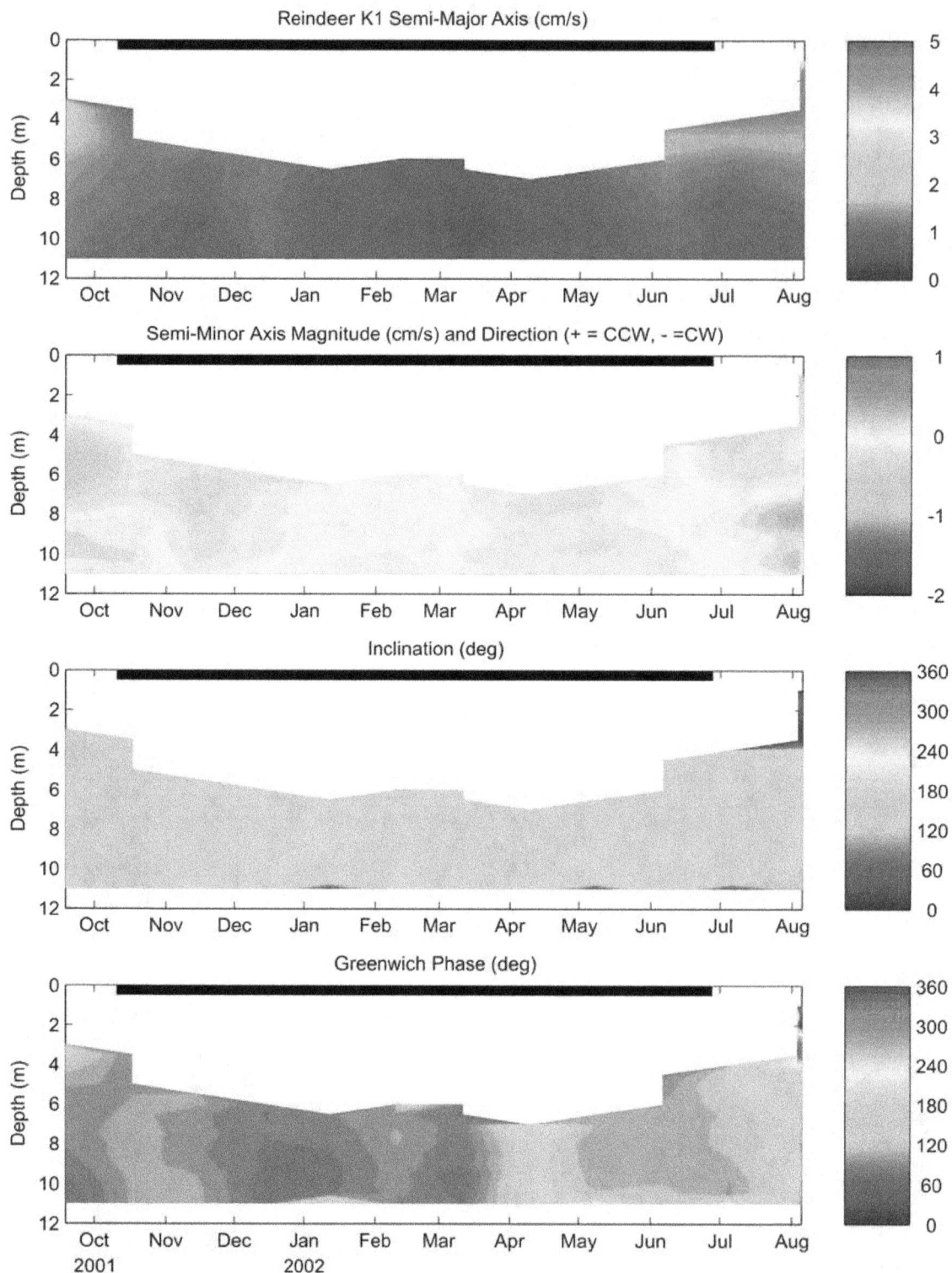

Figure ☐☐ K_1 tidal properties at REINDEER based on 29-day overlapping tidal analyses. The parameters are (from top to bottom) the major axis, minor axis, inclination, and phase. Solid black line indicates landfast ice season.

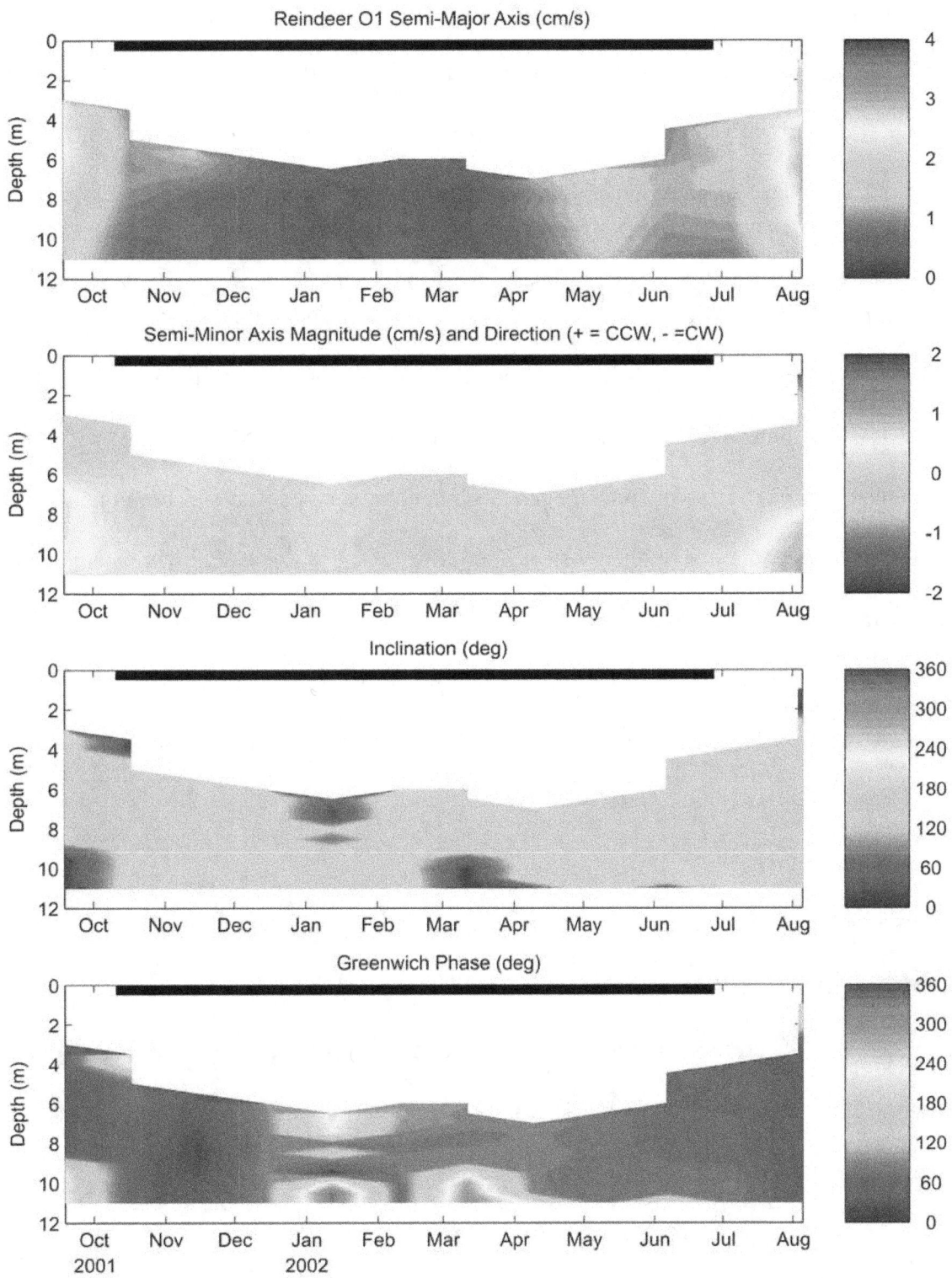

Figure ☐☐ O$_1$ tidal properties at REINDEER based on 29-day overlapping tidal analyses. The parameters are (from top to bottom) the major axis, minor axis, inclination, and phase. Solid black line indicates landfast ice season.

3. Sea level

Time series of the unfiltered and de-meaned sea level (after correcting for the inverted barometer effect) for all years are shown in **Figure** ☐☐Sea-level fluctuations generally range between $\pm$ 0.5 m with a minimum of -1.1m (October 1999) to a maximum of 1.2 m (August 2000). Sea-level fluctuations vary seasonally with rms values being about 0.18 m during the open water season and 0.15 m during the landfast ice period. There are also significant annual and semi-annual sea-level variations, which together account for ~30% of the sea-level variance. Sea-level is a maximum (+0.2 m) in August and a minimum in April-May (-0.2 m) with sub-minima (sub-maxima) occurring in October-December (January-February). The annual range (~0.4 m) cannot be explained by thermosteric (sea-level changes associated with changes in sea-water density) effects, which we estimate are ~0.07 cm. Sea-level fluctuations can be quite large at shorter periods. For example, in April 2000 and in late April 2003 sea level rose by ~1 m and then rapidly decreased by more than 1 m over a 10 day period, with both events coincident with rapid reversals in the along-shore wind stress.

4. Correlations

We turn now to an examination of the seasonal relationship among wind stress, currents, and sea level (η) using both correlations (☐☐☐☐☐☐☐) and dynamical estimates of the terms in linearized along-shelf momentum equation. All correlations are computed after low-pass filtering the currents and sea level time series. Wind stress (rather than wind) is the dynamically important variable and the stresses are computed as:

$$\tau^x = \rho_a C_D W U_W; \qquad \tau^y = \rho_a C_D W V_W;$$

where $\tau^{x\,(y)}$ is the east-west (x) or north-south (y) component of the stress, ρ_a is the air density, C_D is an open water value for the drag coefficient (2.5 x 10^{-3}), W is the wind speed, and U_W (V_W) is the east-west (north-south) component of the wind velocity.

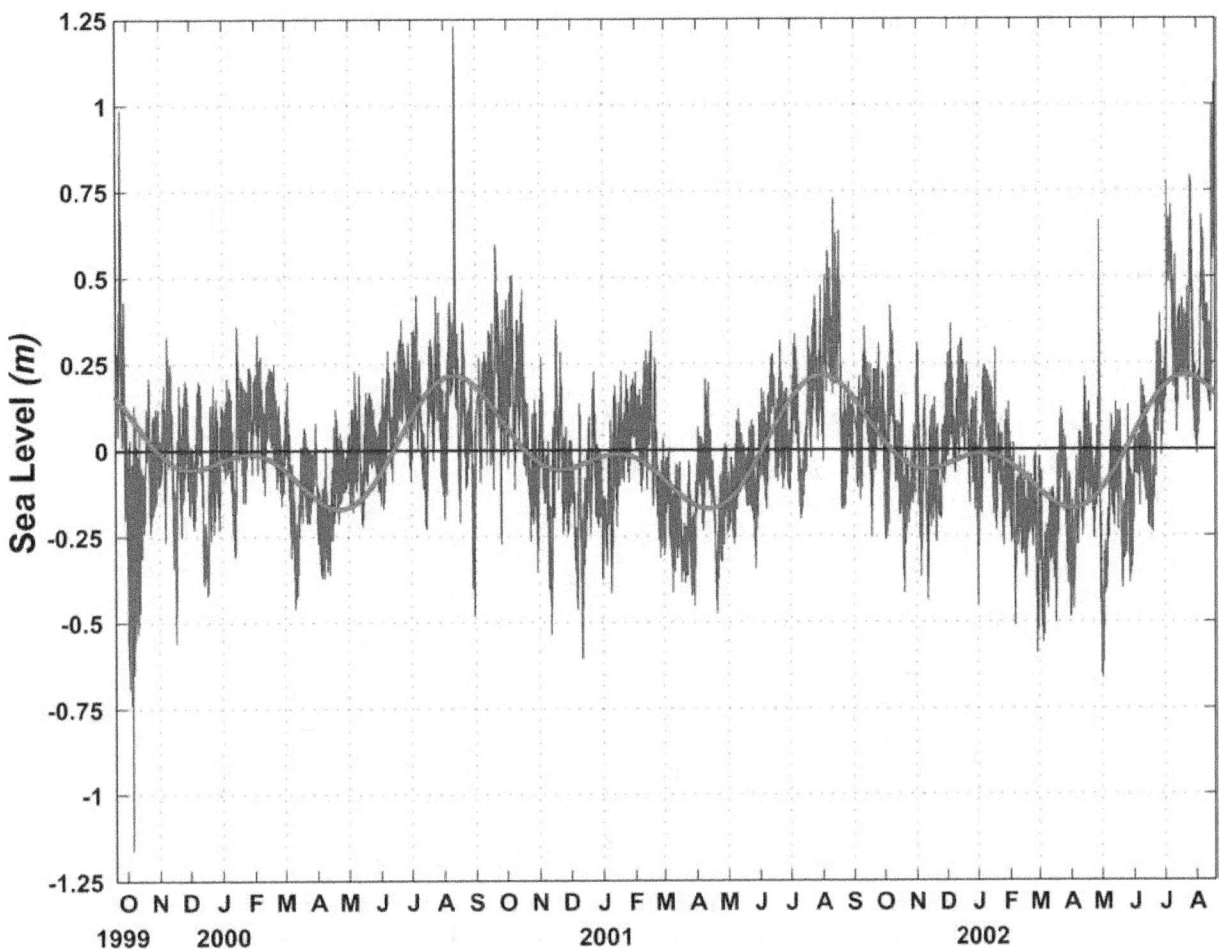

Figure ☐☐ Time series of sea level corrected for the inverted barometer effect from September 1999 – August 2002 (blue line) and the least square harmonic fit to the annual and semi-annual periods (red line).

Both τ^x (☐☐☐☐ ☐☐) and η (☐☐☐☐ ☐☐) are significantly correlated with the along-shore currents at all moorings for all open water periods, although these variables explain generally less than 20 – 50% of the current variance. Correlations between τ^y and along-shelf currents are small and, in general, not statistically significant. Statistically significant positive correlations are found between τ^x and η during the open water period (first row ☐☐ ☐2) with the sign of the

61

correlation consistent with eastward winds inducing a sea-level set-up and westward winds leading to a sea level decrease during the open water season. The correlation is smaller during the 2002 open water season than in the other years, perhaps because of the shorter record length and the absence of large storms during that summer.

☐☐☐ê ☐☐☐Open-water period wind-current correlations. (Italicized entries indicate statistical significance at the α < 0.05 level.).

☐☐ri☐g	☐i☐e ☐eri☐☐	☐☐☐τ^☐☐☐☐r☐	☐☐☐τ^☐☐☐☐r☐
ARGO	2000: (6/30 – 10/20)	*0..68*	0.13
ARGO	2001 (7/4 – 10/13)	*0.50*	*0.33*
ARGO	2002 (6/30 – 8/19)	*0.50*	0.16
DINKUM	2000: (6/30 – 10/22)	*0.71*	0.16
DINKUM	2001: (7/2 – 10/13)	*0.54*	*0.31*
DINKUM	2002 (6/23 – 8/19)	*0.52*	0.09
MCCLURE	2000: (6/30 – 10/22)	*0.65*	0.16
MCCLURE	2001: 7/2 – 8/31	*0.58*	*0.34*
REINDEER	2002: (6/27 – 8/19)	*0.53*	0.15

☐☐☐ê ☐☐☐Open-water period wind-sea level correlations. (Italicized entries indicate statistical significance at the α < 0.05 level.)

☐☐ri☐g	☐i☐e ☐eri☐☐	☐☐☐η☐☐☐r☐
ARGO	2000: (6/30 – 10/20)	*0.66*
ARGO	2001 (7/4 – 10/13)	*0.45*
ARGO	2002 (6/30 – 8/19)	*0.73*
DINKUM	2000: (6/30 – 10/22)	*0.67*
DINKUM	2001: (7/2 – 10/13)	*0.49*
DINKUM	2002 (6/23 – 8/19)	*0.69*
MCCLURE	2000: (6/30 – 10/22)	*0.61*
MCCLURE	2001: 7/2 – 8/31	0.46
REINDEER	2002: (6/27 – 8/19)	0.71

☐☐☐ê ☐2. Wind – sea level correlations for all stations (Italicized entries indicate statistical significance at the α < 0.05 level.)

☐☐☐☐☐ ☐ ☐☐☐☐	2☐☐☐☐☐☐☐ ☐☐☐22	2☐☐☐☐☐2 ☐ ☐☐☐☐☐	2☐2☐☐2☐☐☐☐☐
	0.61	*0.53*	*0.49*
☐☐☐☐F☐☐☐ ☐☐☐	☐☐☐☐☐☐☐☐ ☐ ☐☐☐☐☐☐	☐☐22☐☐☐ ☐ ☐2☐☐☐	☐☐☐☐☐☐☐ ☐ ☐2☐☐2
	0.25	0.28	0.32

In contrast to the open water season, there is no statistically significant correlation between along-shelf currents and τ^x, τ^y (☐☐☐ê ☐☐), or η (☐☐☐ê ☐☐) during the landfast ice period. On the other hand, τ^x and η are both significantly correlated at this time (second row of □□□e □2), although the magnitude of these correlations is about one-half that of the open water season. Correlations between along-shore currents and the zonal component of the geostrophic wind at 72.5°N, 147.5°W from National Center for Environmental Prediction (NCEP) forecast models were also computed. These were non-significant during the landfast ice period, but significant (r = 0.7) during the open water period. The correlation between along-shore currents and the Deadhorse-Pt. Barrow atmospheric pressure difference was significant (r ~ .26) in both seasons, although the correlation explains <10% of the current variance.

□□□e □□ Landfast ice season wind-current correlations. (None are statistically significant at the α < 0.05 level.)

□ □□ri□g	□i□e □eri□□	□□□τ□ □ □□r□	□□□τ□ □ □□r□
ARGO	99/10/15 – 00/6/30	-0.01	0.09
ARGO	00/10/20 – 01/7/4	-0.06	0.21
ARGO	01/10/13 – 02/6/30	0.11	0.15
DINKUM	99/10/15 – 00/6/30	0.07	0.11
DINKUM	00/10/20 – 01/7/4	-0.04	.21
DINKUM	01/10/13 – 02/06/23	0.10	0.14
MCCLURE	99/10/15 – 00/6/30	-0.06	0.05
MCCLURE	00/10/20 – 01/7/4	-0.05	0.17
REINDEER	01/10/10 – 02/6/27	0.12	0.14

□□□e □□□Landfast ice season sea-level-current correlations. (None are statistically significant at the α < 0.05 level.)

□ □□ri□g	□i□e □eri□□	□
ARGO	99/10/15 – 00/6/30	0.07
ARGO	00/10/20 – 01/7/4	0.12
ARGO	01/10/13 – 02/6/30	0.12
DINKUM	99/10/15 – 00/6/30	0.15
DINKUM	00/10/20 – 01/7/4	0.13
DINKUM	01/10/13 – 02/06/23	0.09
MCCLURE	99/10/15 – 00/6/30	-0.01
MCCLURE	00/10/20 – 01/7/4	0.09
REINDEER	01/10/10 – 02/6/27	0.07

The absence of a significant wind-current correlation contrasts with *Aagaard's* [1984] suggestion that currents on the inner shelf were correlated with the winds during the landfast ice period. His conclusion, however, was based on visual inspection of wind and current records from two 3-week current meter records collected under the landfast ice in water depths of 27 and 38 m, approximately 35 km northeast of the DINKUM mooring. There are two possible reasons for the difference. First, his measurements might have coincided with a period when winds and currents were roughly correlated and such periods times are evident upon inspection of our data set. On the other hand, Aagaard's measurements were made much closer to the edge of the landfast ice, perhaps within one or two deformation radii (say within ~10 km), so that the offshore winds influenced the currents near but inshore of the ice edge at his locations, but perhaps not at locations further inshore. The latter is plausible based upon results from simple idealized numerical circulation models we have begun conducting of the landfast ice zone and offshore region for the Beaufort Sea. We find that the imposition of an alongshore wind stress over the region seaward of the landfast ice produces an along-ice edge jet whose inshore extent is $<$~10 km. We also find that the flow inshore of the jet reverses, although the nearshore flow is small (~1cm-s^{-1}). The flow reversal occurs because the sea-level slope reverses at the ice edge due to the large wind stress curl imposed at the offshore boundary of the ice edge. This curl induces Ekman suction, which lowers or raises the sea level at the ice edge relative to the sea-level beneath the ice. Hence a current reversal develops beneath the landfast ice and inshore of the ice edge. Although our model results are preliminary (and assume no frictional coupling between the ice and the under-ice flow at this stage), they suggest a cross-shore reversal in the along-shelf flow across the landfast ice boundary could develop.

5. Dynamics

We now examine the vertically integrated along-shore momentum balance at subtidal and seasonal time scales using data from the moorings and wind stresses as calculated above. The vertically integrated, linearized, along-shore momentum equation is:

$$\frac{\partial U}{\partial t} = -g\frac{\partial \eta}{\partial x} + \frac{\tau_s^x}{\rho H} - \frac{\tau_b^x}{\rho H} \qquad (\square)$$
$$\text{(a)} \qquad \text{(b)} \quad \text{(c)} \quad \text{(d)}$$

where U is the vertically averaged along-shore velocity component, g the gravitational acceleration, H the water depth, ρ the density, and τ^x the stress in the along-shore direction. The subscripts "s" and "b" refer to the stress at the surface and bottom, respectively. The equation states that local accelerations in along-shore velocities (term a) are balanced by the along-shore pressure gradient arising from the along-shore sea level slope (term b) and the vertically integrated effects of surface (term c) and bottom stresses (term d). The bottom stress (τ_b^x) is often parameterized by a linear stress law, $\tau_b^x = \rho r U$, with r, the resistance coefficient being~10^{-4} m-s^{-1} [*Csanady*, 1981; *Lentz*, 1994]. We assumed that the non-linear terms in this force balance are small and we have neglected the effects of wave radiation stresses. The latter arise due to surface gravity waves propagating obliquely onshore and these stresses can be a substantial momentum source in shallow water (<5m) during storms [*Lentz et al.*, 1999]. Although wave radiation stresses are absent during the landfast ice period, they might occasionally be important during the open water period. We believe that these stresses are likely small because the energy of onshore propagating waves is probably dissipated (to some extent) along the barrier islands and shoals girding the offshore boundary of Stefannsson Sound. In summer, τ_s^x is the surface wind stress, whereas in winter it arises due to frictional coupling between the ocean and the

65

underside of the immobile landfast ice. Consequently, both the sea bottom and the underside of the ice exert a frictional stress against the along-shore flow during the landfast ice season, whereas during the open water season bottom and surface stresses oppose one another. For present purposes we assume that the underice stress can be parameterized in the same manner as the bottom stress, e.g. ($\tau_b^x = \tau_s^x = \rho r U$) with $r \sim 10^{-4}$ m-s^{-1} for both stress terms. For reasons to be discussed later, our choice of r for the resistance coefficient between ice and water might not be valid. However, in the absence of the necessary observations, we assume that it is of the same magnitude as the bottom resistance coefficient. With this assumption, equation 1 becomes:

$$\frac{\partial U}{\partial t} = -g\frac{\partial \eta}{\partial x} - \frac{2rU}{H} \qquad (2)$$

We computed all terms in equations 1 and 2 except the along-shore sea level slope, which is estimated as the residual. The results are shown using data from DINKUM for the 2000 and 2001 open water seasons (**Figure□□ □□ □**) and for each landfast ice season (**Figure□□ □□**). Results using other moorings are similar and not shown.

In both seasons balance is primarily achieved among the stresses and along-shelf pressure gradient, with the local acceleration term ($\partial U / \partial t$) typically being 10^{-6} or smaller and an order of magnitude smaller than the other terms. In both seasons the along-shelf pressure gradients imply along-shore sea level slopes of ± 10 cm/100 km. If these slopes extend the entire length of the Alaskan Beaufort coast then the sea level difference between Barrow and the US-Canada boundary can be as large as 0.5 m, which is easily detected with pressure gauges. The average along-shore velocity over the landfast ice period is virtually negligible implying that the there is no mean sea level slope during this season. In general, the along-shelf sea level gradients are about twice as large during the open water season than during the landfast ice period. We emphasize that the estimates of the winter along-shore sea-level gradients are uncertain, however, because of uncertainty in the ice-water frictional coupling.

Nevertheless, the presence of sub-tidal underice flows requires an along-shore sea level slope. How these slopes originate is not clear, however, although several possibilities exist. First, sea level fluctuations might be induced on the western shelf near Barrow due to variations in the coastal current that drains the Chukchi Sea through Barrow Canyon [*Weingartner et al.*, 1998; accepted]. If this were the primary forcing for the underice flows, we would expect a stronger correlation between the underice currents and the NCEP wind fields, since currents in the Chukchi Sea are strongly correlated with these winds [*Weingartner et al.*, 1998; accepted]. We would also expect that the variance in current and along-shore sea level would be greater in late fall-early winter than in late winter as these authors found for the flow in Barrow Canyon. Second, fluctuating along-shore coastal sea-level gradients can be established by time-varying divergences in the along-shelf wind field. Third, spatial variations in the underice friction associated with the complex deformation field of the sea ice might establish cross-shelf flows that alter the along-shelf pressure field [*Trowbridge et al.*, 1998]. Finally, remotely forced continental shelf waves could also affect the along-shore pressure gradient. These waves would be forced by wind stress variations to the west (as far west as the East Siberian Sea, for example) of our measurement site. This possibility cannot be discounted, but is beyond the scope of the present study.

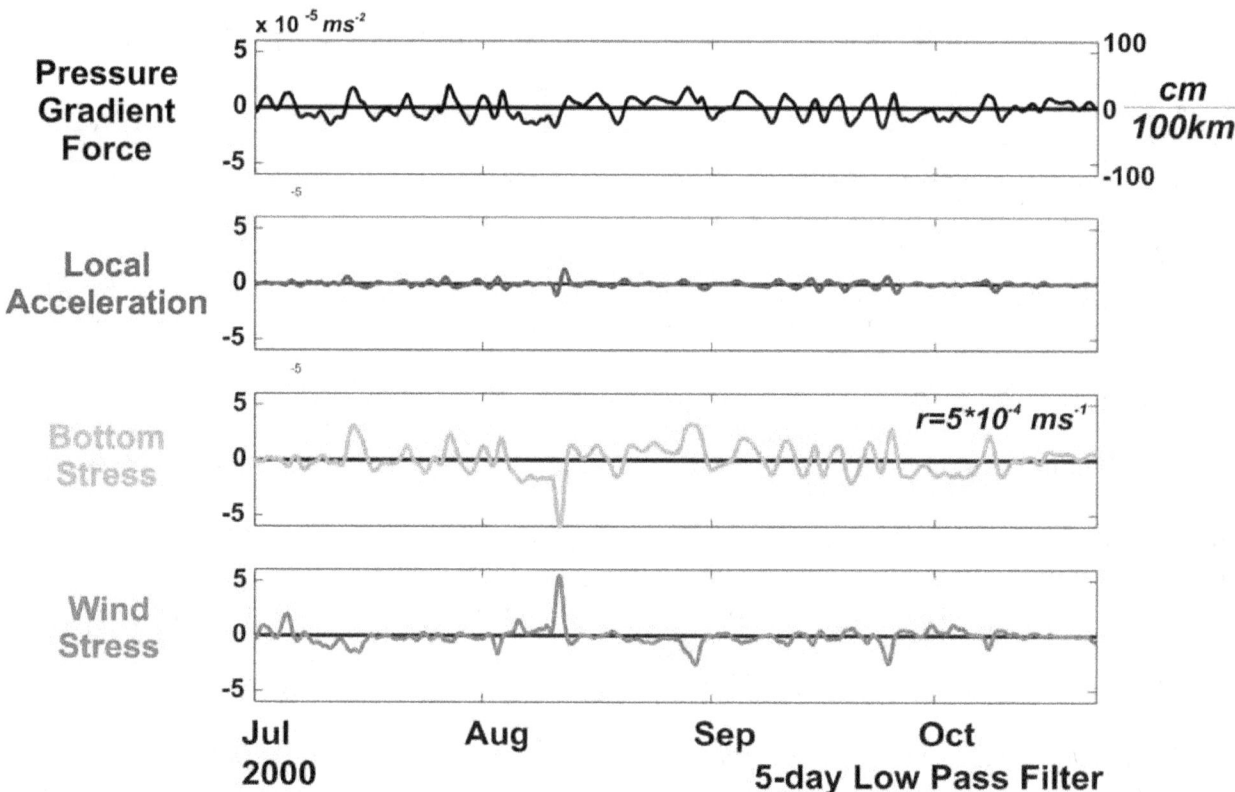

Figure ☐☐ Time series of the terms in the vertically integrated along-shelf momentum equation for the 2000 open water season using data from DINKUM.

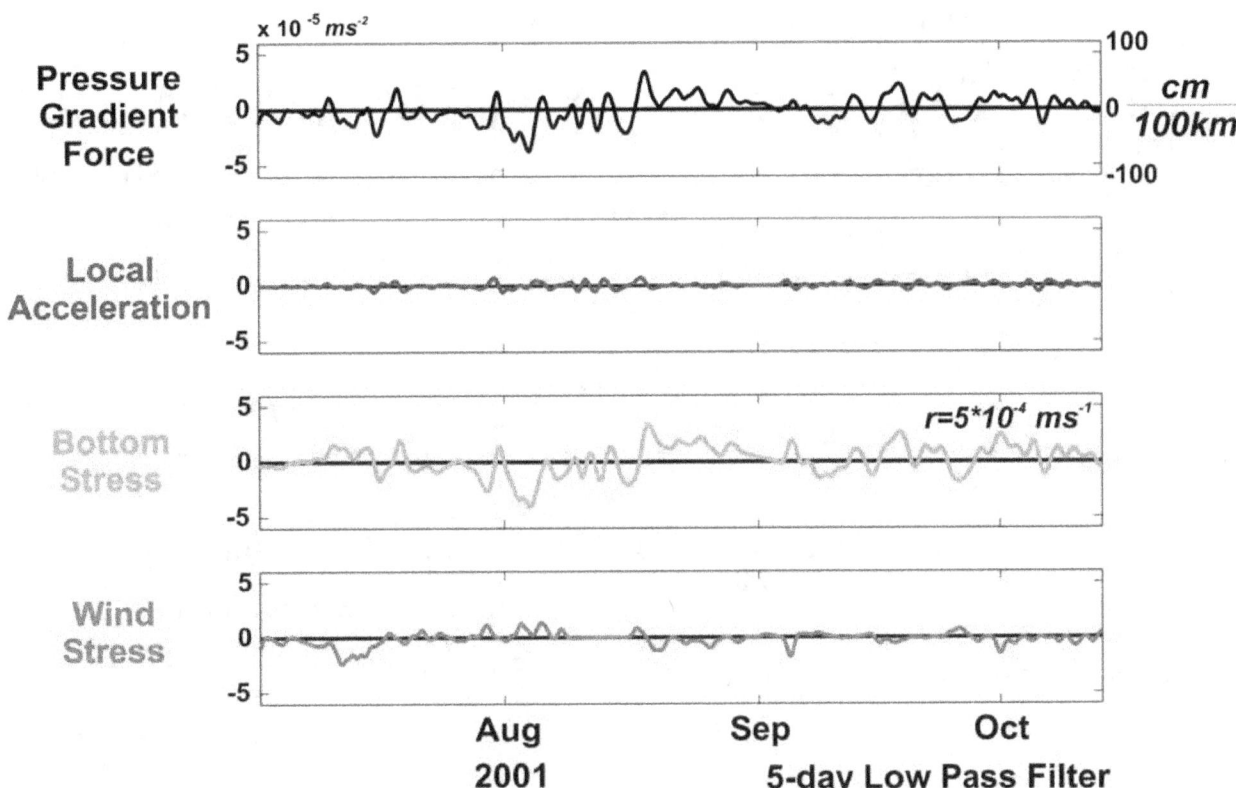

Figure ☐☐☐ Time series of the terms in the vertically integrated along-shelf momentum equation for the 2001 open water season using data from DINKUM.

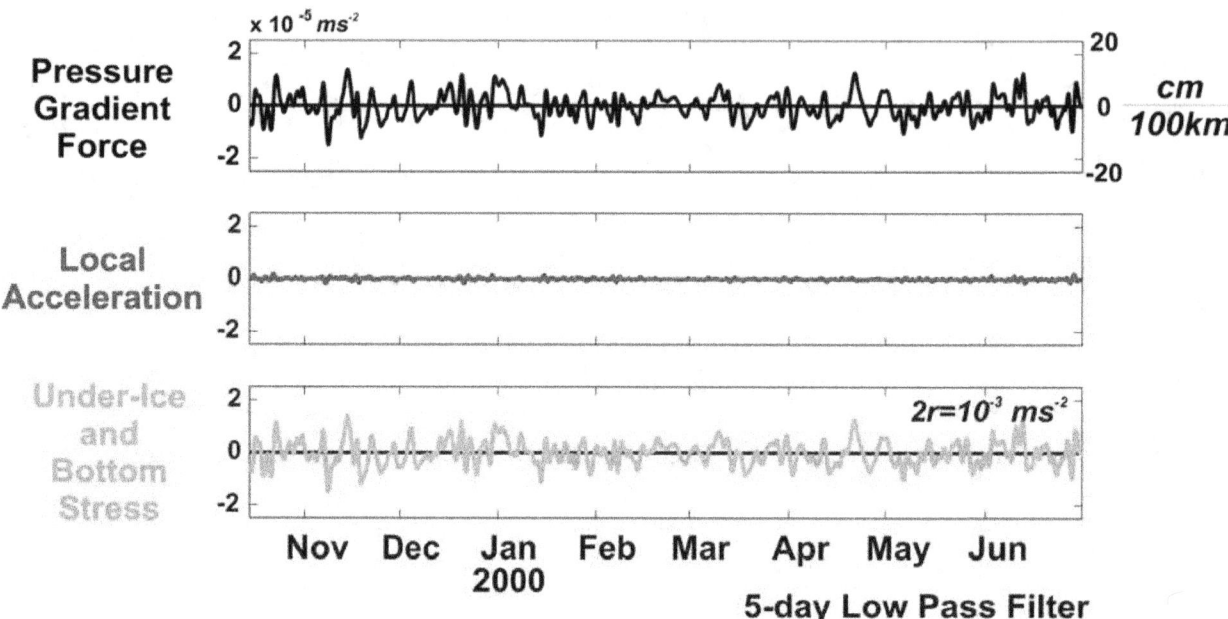

Figure ⬚⬚ Time series of the terms in the vertically integrated along-shelf momentum equation for the 2000 – 2001 landfast ice season using data from DINKUM.

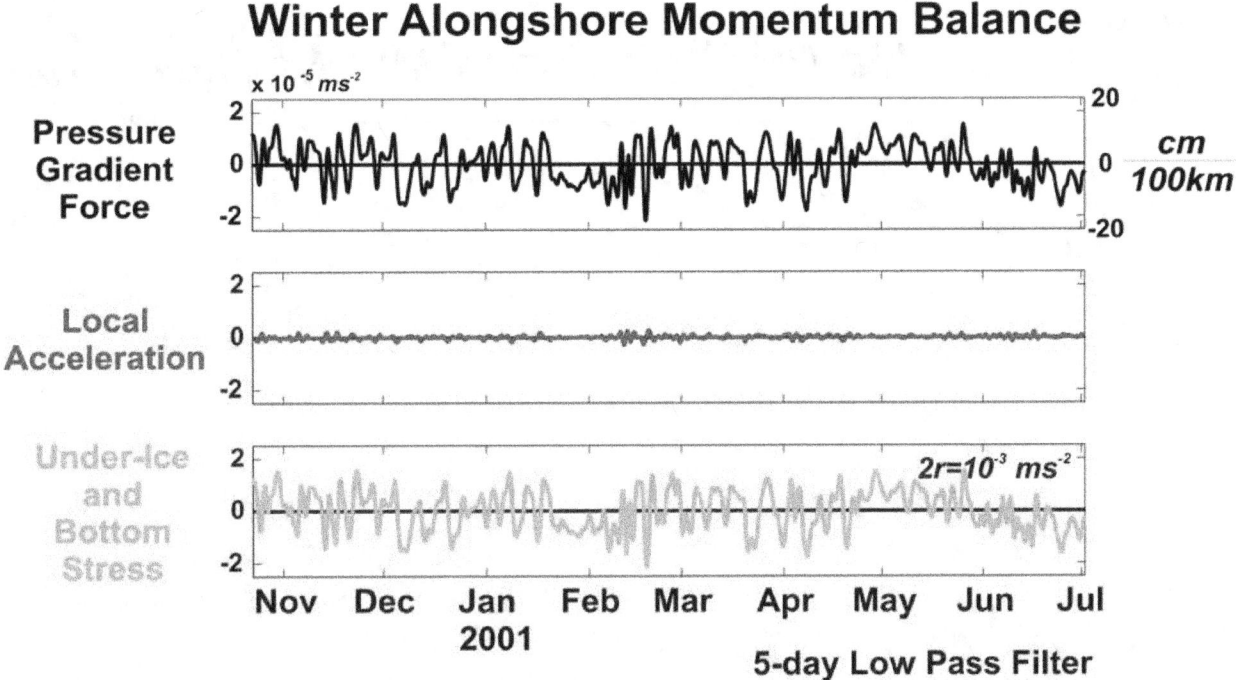

Figure ☐☐Time series of the terms in the vertically integrated along-shelf momentum equation for the 2001 – 2002 landfast ice season using data from DINKUM.

Winter Alongshore Momentum Balance

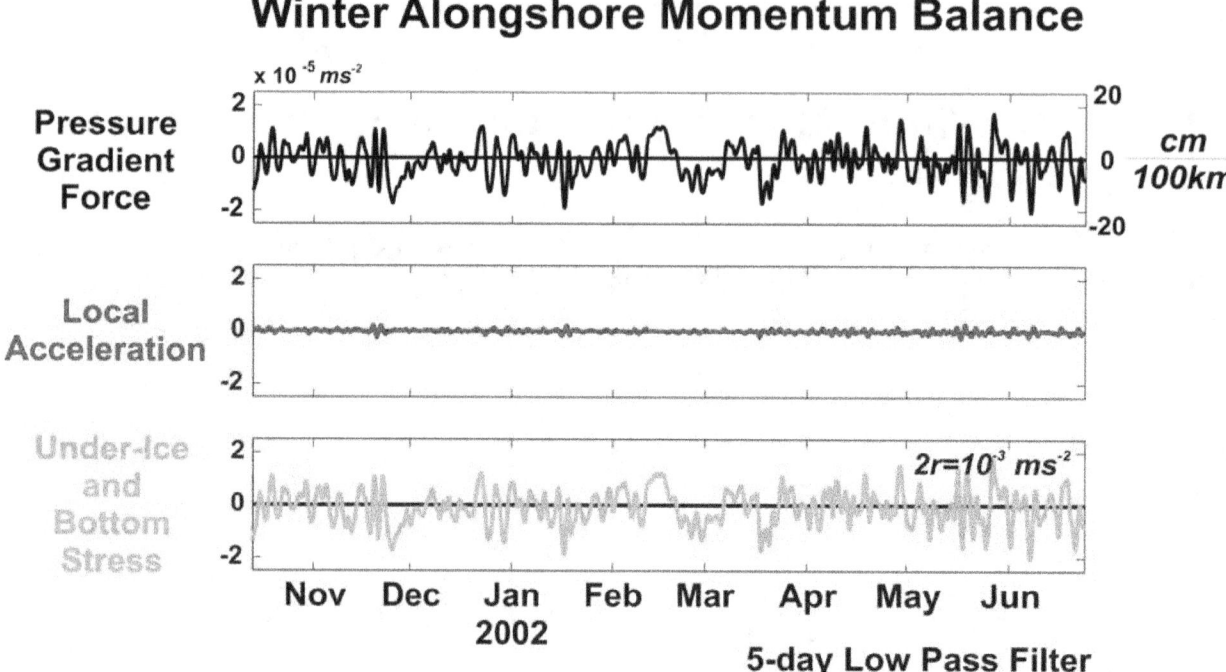

Figure ☐☐☐Time series of the terms in the vertically integrated along-shelf momentum equation for the 2001 – 2002 landfast ice season using data from DINKUM.

6. *Temperature, salinity, transmissivity, fluorescence*

Water property parameters also vary throughout the year in accordance with the development and retreat of sea ice. The annual cycles of temperature (T) and salinity (S) are shown for each mooring (with high quality data) in **Figure 2** At each location the annual temperature cycle consists of maximum near-bottom temperatures that range from $5 - 2^{\circ}C$ in summer and fall, followed by a rapid (1 – 2 week) collapse to the freezing point ($\sim-1.7^{\circ}C$) (usually in early October), after which temperatures remain near-freezing until late June or early July. At that time, temperatures slowly increase and reach about $0^{\circ}C$ by late July after the ice melts. Salinity varies from 14 through 32 through the open water season, with the lowest salinities observed immediately following the decay of the landfast ice and in the aftermath of sufficiently strong winds that mix the water column. After the ice forms in October, salinities increase and attain values of 34 – 35 by January due to the expulsion of salt from growing sea ice. Thereafter, salinities remain relatively constant through winter and spring before slowly starting to decrease in June. Following the removal of ice and the first significant wind-mixing event, salinities rapidly decrease as a consequence of mixing of low-salinity ice meltwater and the river plume (discussed in Section V).

Transmissivity also shows a strong seasonal cycle. During late summer and fall it varies due to stirring by the winds and currents, but generally decreases to very low values at about the time of rapid ice formation in early October. The low values are due to turbulent mixing of the water column brought about by winds and cooling and freezing that extend over the entire water column. The high suspended sediment levels in the water column during freeze-up suggest that much sediment is included into the landfast ice matrix during the vigorous production period. The incorporation of sediments into sea-ice has bearing on oil dispersal because the sea ice represents a potential vehicle by which oiled sediments can be subsequently transported out of the region. However, that transport would be delayed until the following summer during and after break-up. Either the sediment-laden ice will be advected out of the region or will melt *in-situ* and release its oiled sediments back into the water. Transmissivity values remain relatively high through winter although the data suggests periods of moderate suspended sediments followed by clearer water masses. Winter periods of moderately low transmissivity might, in fact, be a sampling artifact because the transmissometer was inclined to the horizontal on the mooring frame. Thus, sediment might have accumulated on the lens during periods of low flow and then be cleansed when current speeds increased. Although there is some uncertainty in the winter transmissivity record, there is a consistently large decrease in transmissivity in early June of each year, coincident with the spring freshet when rivers are carrying a heavy suspended sediment load. This load sinks to the seabed under the landfast ice because there is little energy available for mixing in the water column. Once the ice retreats, the near-bottom suspended sediment load remains relatively low until vigorous storms mix sediment back into the water column where it is advected by wind-driven currents.

Fluorescence provides a qualitative measure of the chlorophyll content in the water. These values are always low except in late July or August after the ice has disappeared and transmissivity levels have risen above the post freshet minimum.

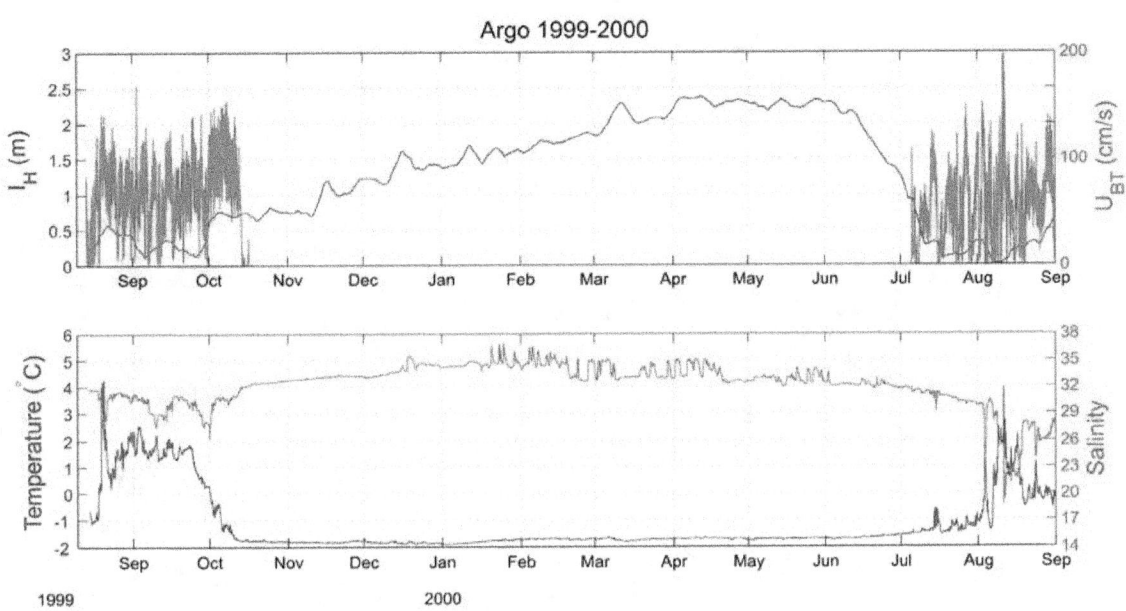

Figure 2 Ice thickness and bottom track velocity (upper panel) and temperature and salinity (lower panel) at ARGO during the 1999 – 2000 deployment.

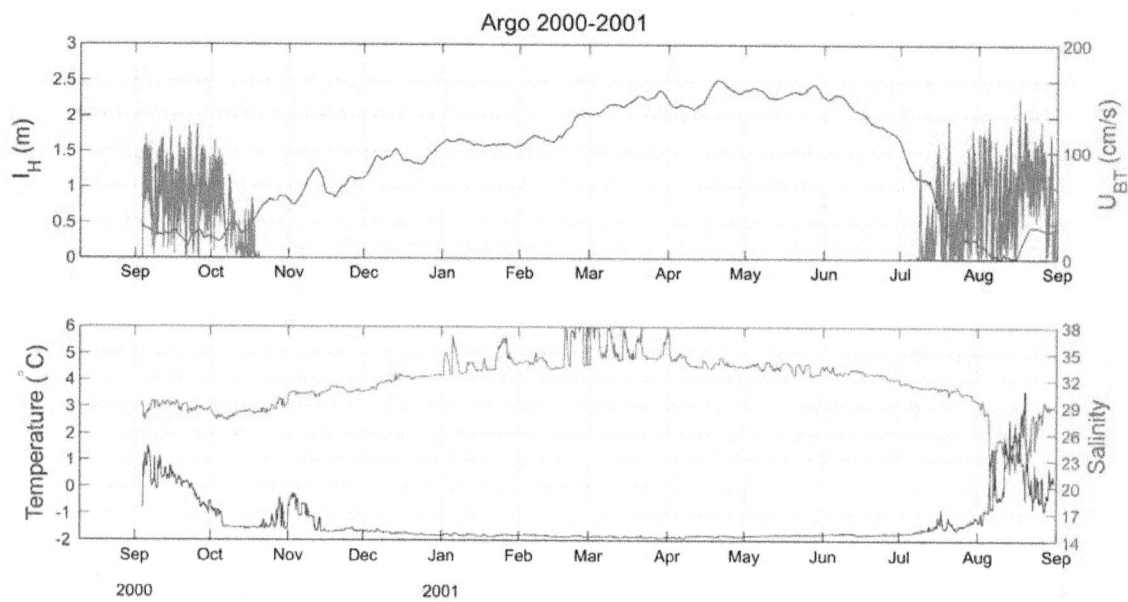

Figure ☐☐☐Ice thickness and bottom track velocity (upper panel) and temperature and salinity (lower panel) at ARGO during the 2000 – 2001 deployment.

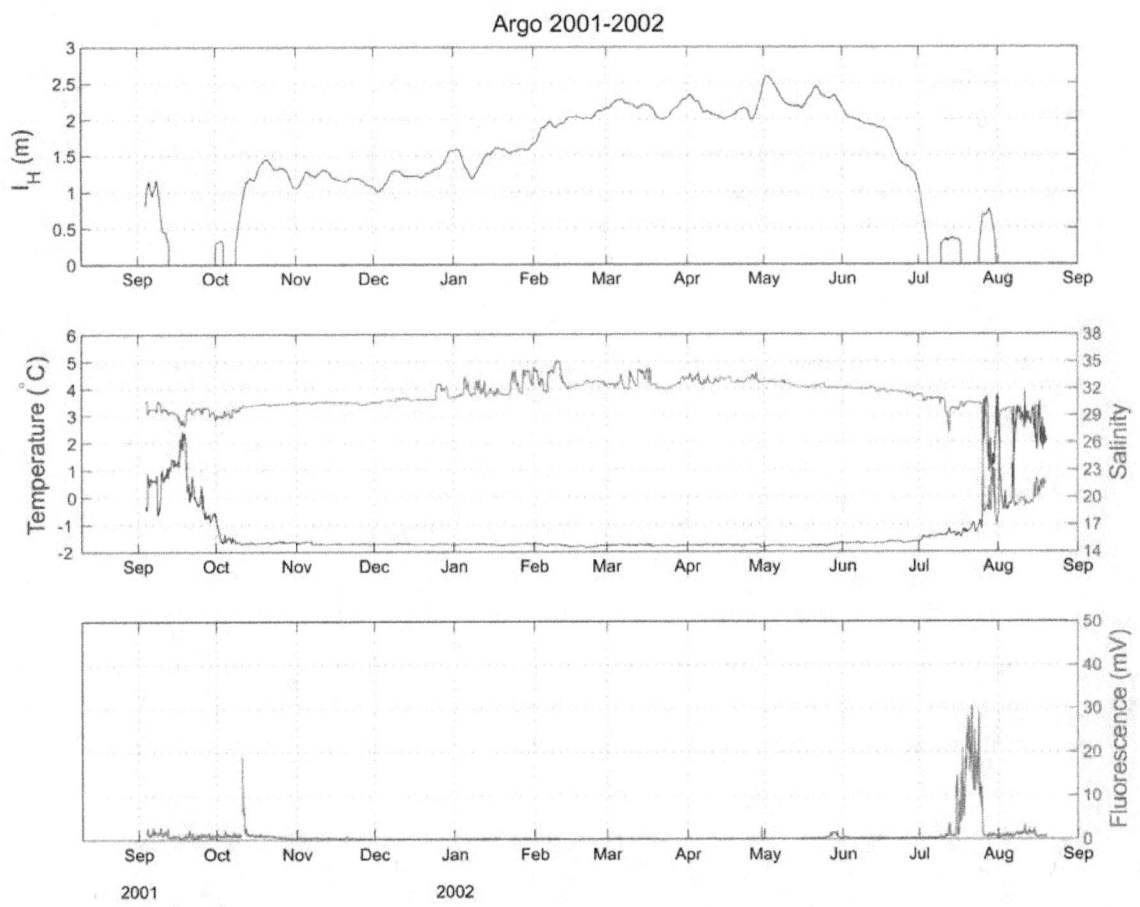

Figure □□Ice thickness (upper panel), temperature and salinity (middle panel) and fluorescence (lower panel) at ARGO during the 2001 – 2002 deployment.

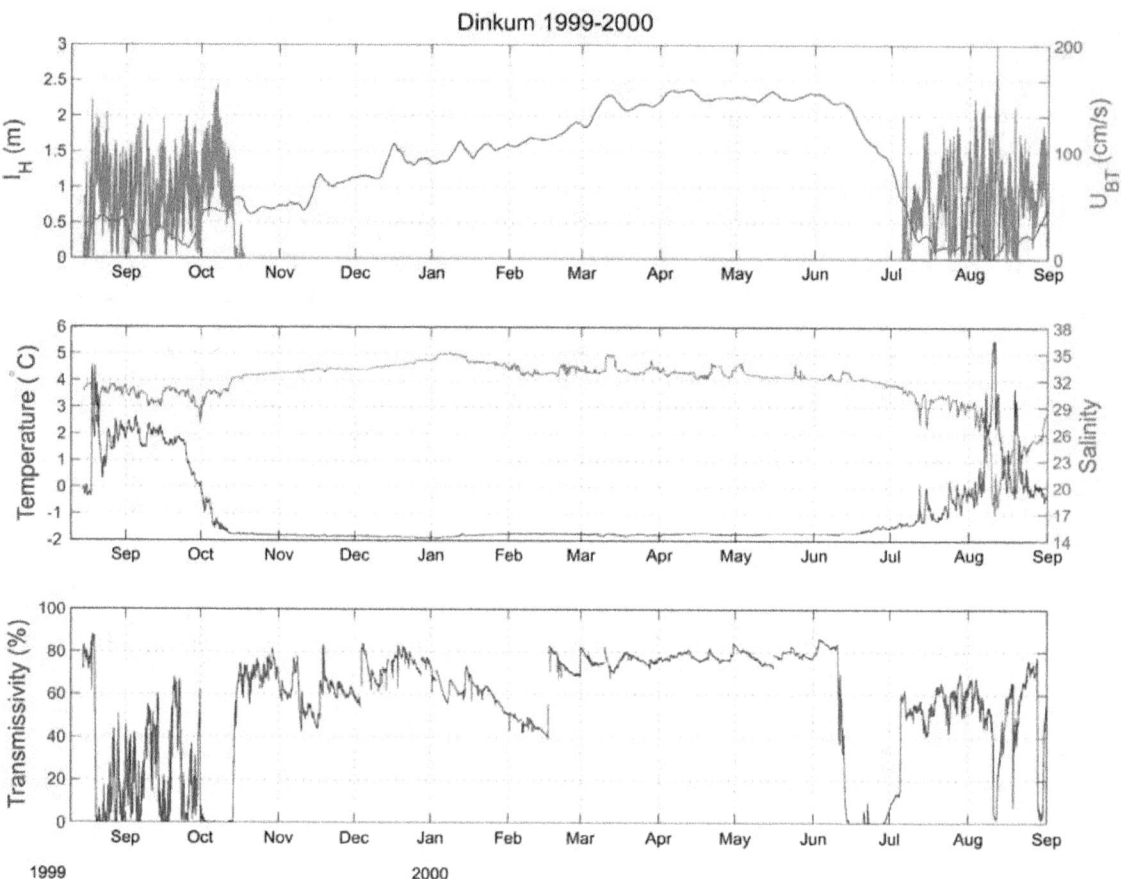

Figure 45. Ice thickness (upper panel), temperature and salinity (middle panel) and transmissivity (lower panel) at DINKUM during the 1999 - 2000 deployment.

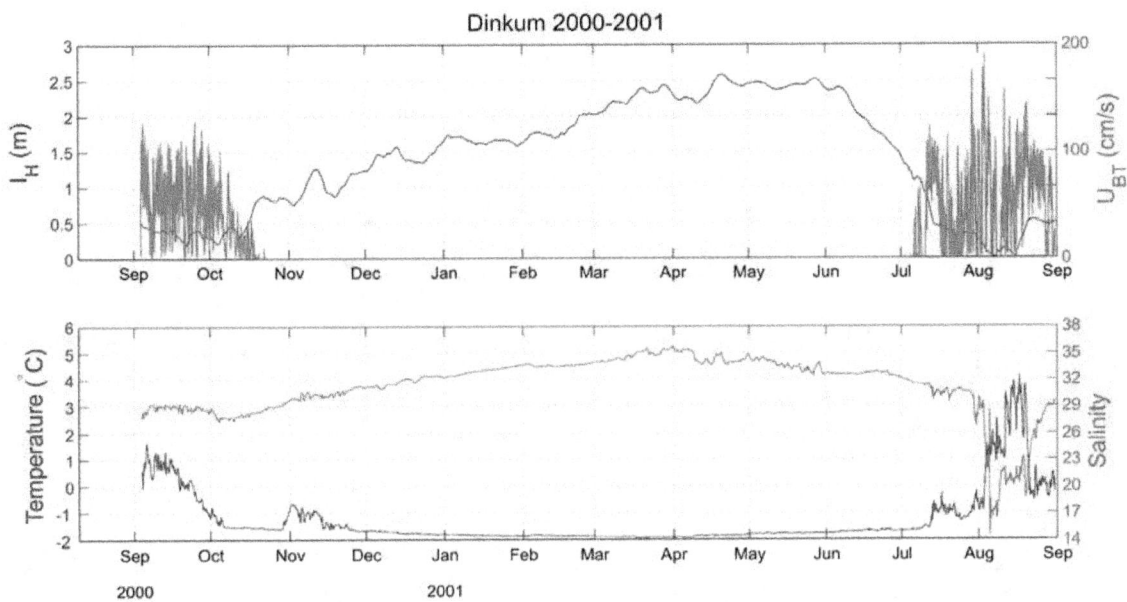

Figure 4 Ice thickness (upper panel) and temperature and salinity (lower panel) at DINKUM during the 2000 - 20001 deployment.

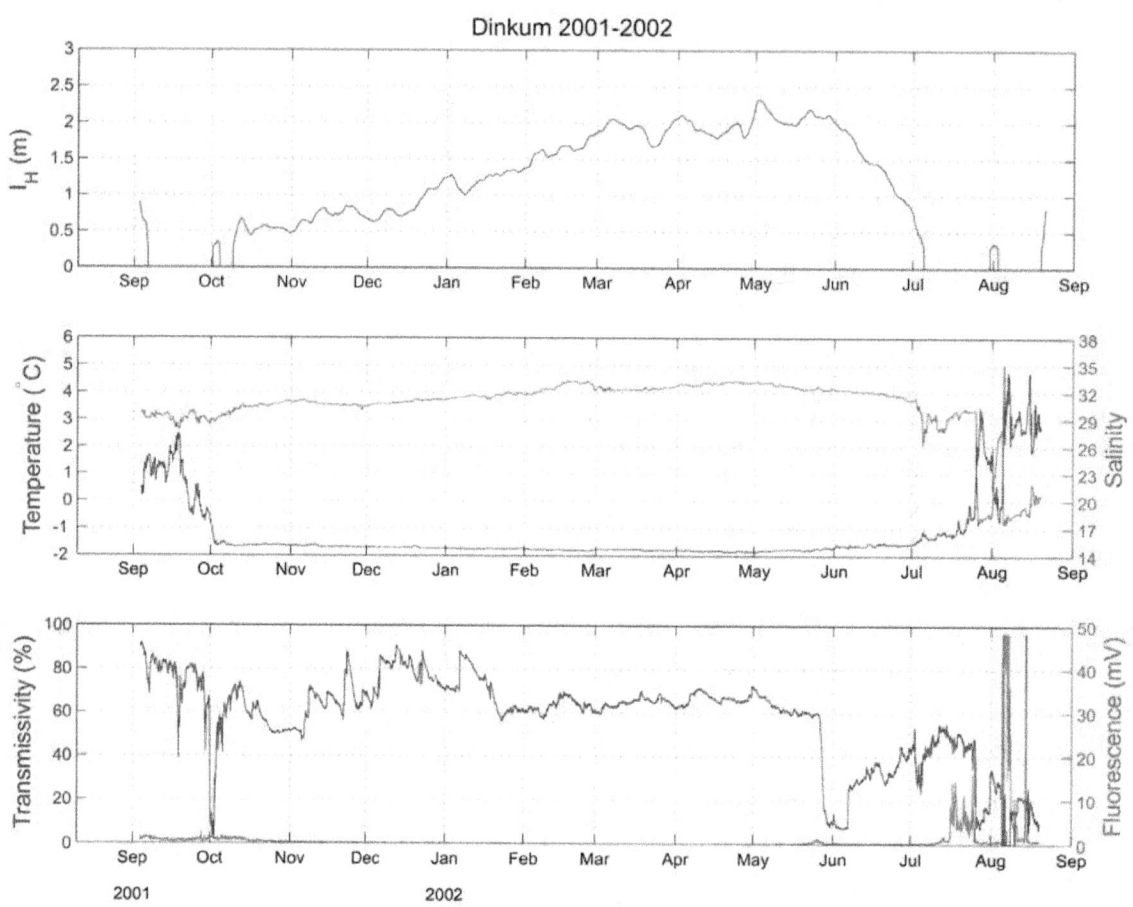

Figure 4□ Ice thickness (upper panel), temperature and salinity (middle panel) and transmissivity and flourescence (lower panel) at DINKUM during the 2001 - 2000 deployment.

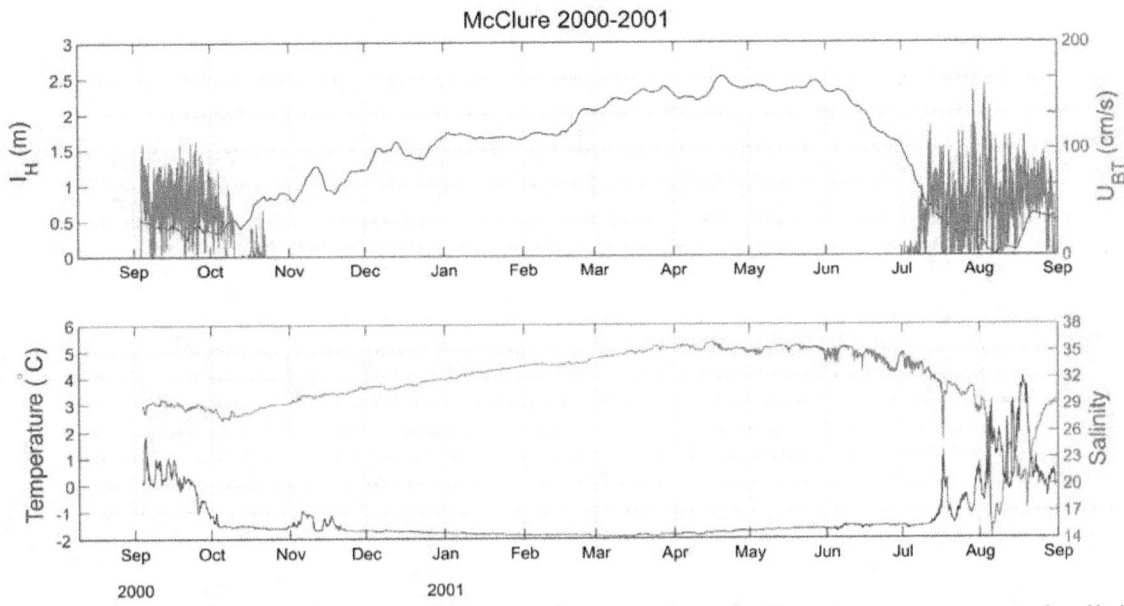

Figure 4 Ice thickness and bottom-track velocity (upper panel) and temperature and salinity (lower panel) at MCCLURE during the 2000 - 2001 deployment.

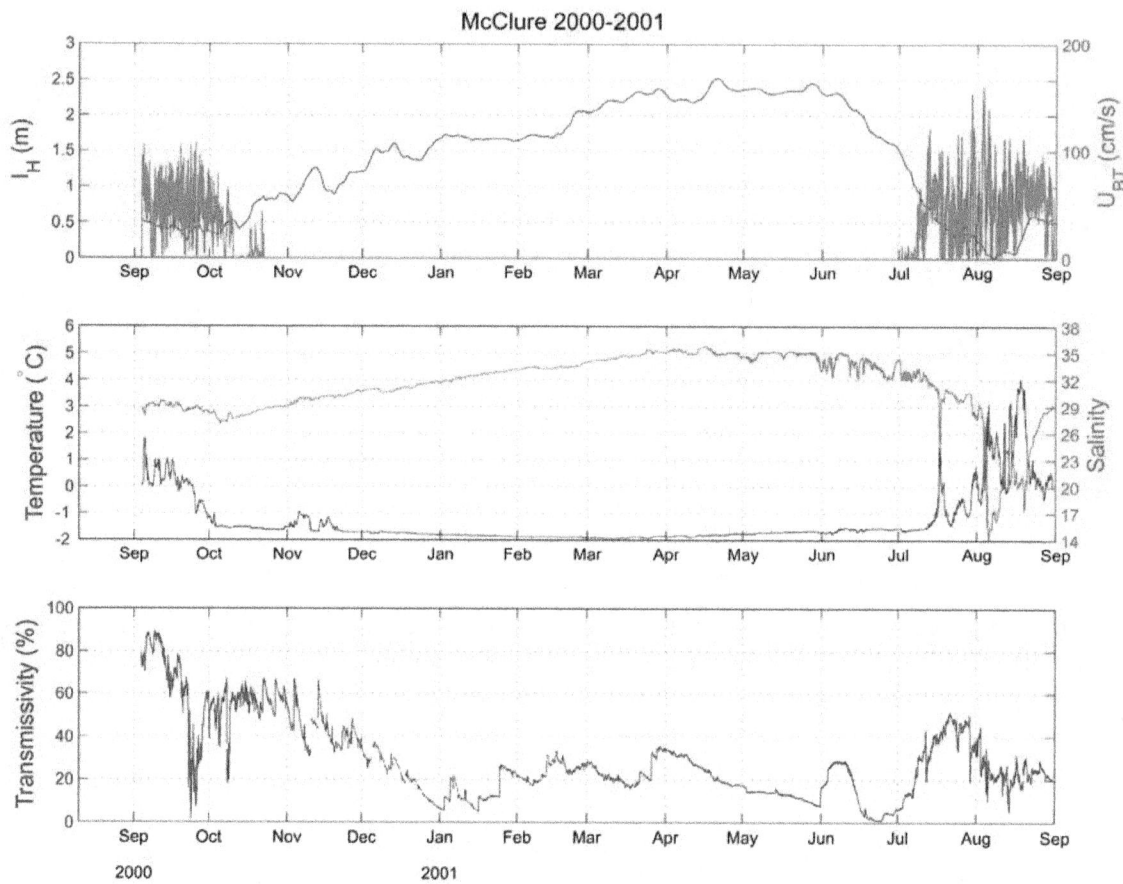

Figure 4 Ice thickness and bottom-track velocity (upper panel), temperature and salinity (middle panel) and transmissivity at MCCLURE during the 2001 - 2002 deployment.

Figure 5 shows in detail the relationship between Sagavanirktok River discharge, transmissivity, ice thickness, currents and current shears from May through June from mooring DINKUM in 2000. Prior to the onset of discharge, all parameters are relatively constant and typical of winter conditions. However, once the freshet reaches its maximum on June 9, the transmissivity and ice thickness rapidly decrease, relatively large cross-shore flows (of up to 10 cm-s^{-1}) are initiated, and vertical shears increase. Rapid sea-ice ablation occurs due both to strong solar heating and to the rapid decrease in albedo of the ice surface by melt water ponds and/or the spreading of turbid river water over the surface of the ice *Searcy et al.* [1996].

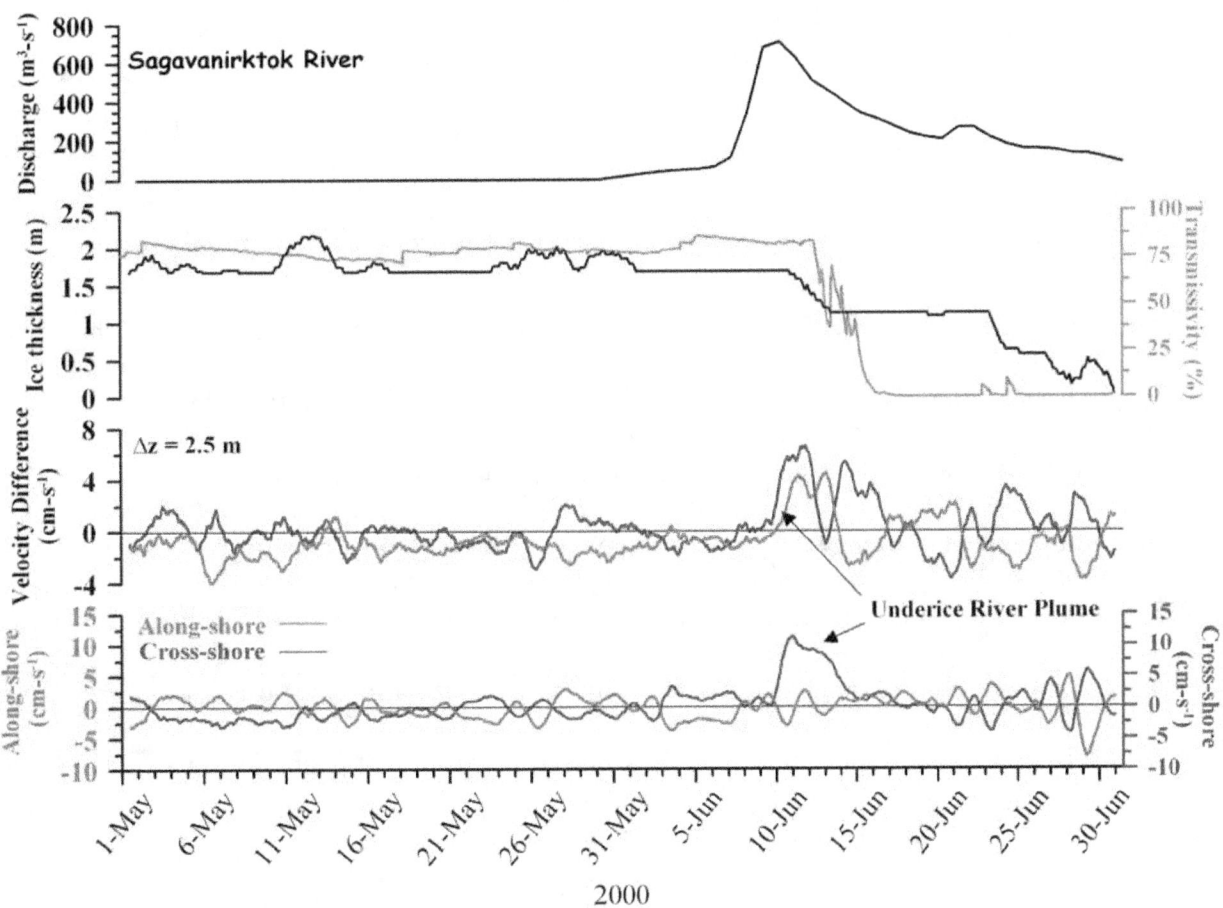

Figure 5 May through June time series of (from top to bottom) Sagavanirktok River discharge, ice thickness (black), transmissivity (green), cross- and along-shore velocity shear, and cross- and along-shore velocities. Along-shore (cross-shore) components are ref (blue).

E. Freshwater Runoff Influence

In this section we further explore the influence that freshwater runoff exerts on the inner shelf's density structure and circulation field. During river breakup a significant fraction of the river runoff flows beneath the landfast ice where it establishes a strongly stratified water column, with salinity accounting for most of the stratification (**Figure 5**). Salinities increase by ~25 m^{-1} across the halocline, while temperature decreases by 1.5 $^{\circ}$C m^{-1} (**Figure 5**) and transmissivity by 80% m^{-1} (**Figure 5**). The inner shelf will remain highly stratified until sufficient turbulent energy is supplied to the water column to mix it vertically. This is evident from the bulk Richardson number:

$$Ri = \frac{g}{\rho}\left(\frac{\partial \rho}{\partial z}\right) \Big/ \left[\left(\frac{\partial u}{\partial z}\right)^2 + \left(\frac{\partial v}{\partial z}\right)^2\right]$$

where $\frac{\partial \rho}{\partial z}$ is the vertical density gradient and the denominator is the square of the vertical gradient of horizontal velocity. $Ri \sim 325$ for typical values of the gradients of underice shear and density observed during river runoff in summer. These values are substantially greater than the range of 1 - 10 typical of weak and moderately stratified shelf conditions and much larger than the value of 0.25 where mixing occurs. The large Richardson number also implies that interfacial stresses are small so that most of the momentum imparted by the wind stress, once the ice has receded will be confined to the plume. This has important implications for the subsequent spreading of the plume after the landfast ice retreats. For example, if we assume that the wind stress is confined to a strongly stratified 2 m thick plume, a weak but upwelling favorable wind speed of 2 m s^{-1} would transport the plume seaward at ~5 cm s^{-1} (~5 km day^{-1}). Such winds are not unrealistic for the nearshore Beaufort Sea in summer where the mean winds are westward (and upwelling favorable) due to the sea breeze effect.

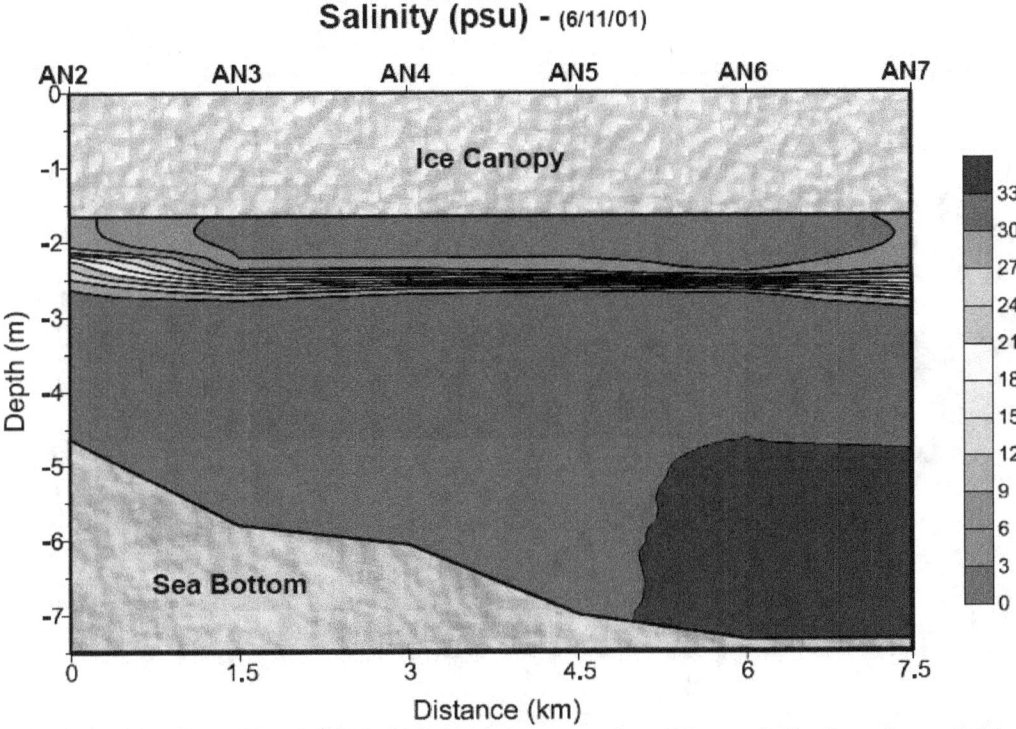

Figure 51. Salinity along the DINKUM 2001 transect (see Figure 3 for location of this transect).

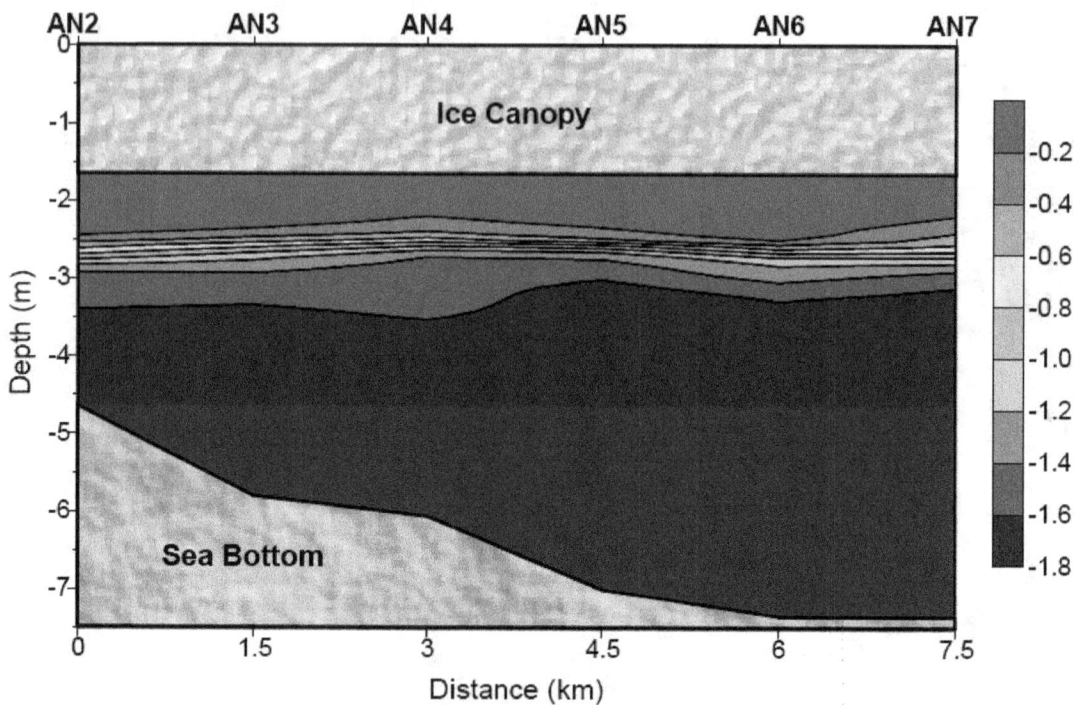

Figure 52. Temperature along the DINKUM 2001 transect (see Figure 3 for location of this transect).

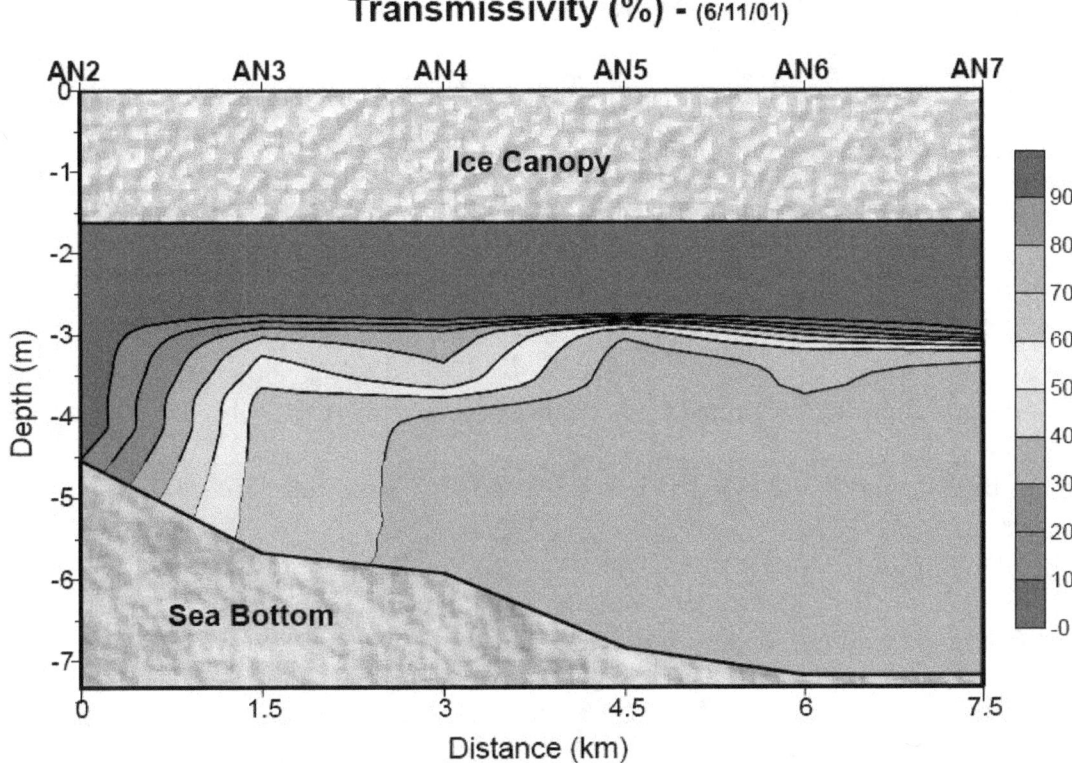

Figure 53. Transmissivity along the DINKUM 2001 transect (see Figure 3 for location of this transect).

The offshore velocity of the plume is comparable to the 6 cm s[-1] alongshore speed a surface oil slick would have assuming it moves at 2% of the wind speed. Although simplified, this example suggests that the effects of stratification and vertical mixing cannot be ignored in oil spill trajectory models for the nearshore Beaufort Sea in summer.

How rapidly the stratification erodes depends upon the strength of the winds once the ice has retreated or becomes mobile, since wind is the primary agent for supplying mixing energy for the water column. We determine the work required to mix from the potential energy of the water column:

$$M = \frac{1}{h} \int_{-h}^{0} (\rho(z) - \bar{\rho}) gz \, dz \qquad (4)$$

87

where g is the gravitational acceleration, $\rho(z)$ is the density at depth z, and $\bar{\rho}$ is the mean density

of the water column. The winds are the sole source of mixing energy because the currents (tidal

and subtidal) have insufficient shear to overcome the large density gradient. We estimate the

time required to vertical mix the water column from *Denman and Miyake's* [1973] relationship:

$$\frac{\partial E}{\partial t} \cong \frac{\rho_a m C_D U_{10}^3}{h} \tag{5}$$

where ($\partial E/\partial t$) is the rate of working by the wind on the water column, ρ_a is the air density (1.29

kg m^{-3}), m is an efficiency factor and C_D is the drag coefficient (both $\sim 10^{-3}$), h is the water depth

(5.6 m for the CTD profiles shown in **Figure 5**□) and U_{10}^3 is the cube of the wind speed at 10 m

elevation. Dividing eq. 4 by eq. 5 gives the time required for a *steady* wind to mix the water

column. Complete mixing is achieved in 3 (28) days for constant winds of 6 (3) m s^{-1}. Thus the

structure of the nearshore water column can vary considerably from year to year depending upon

the seasonal evolution of the wind field.

The cross-shore velocities associated with the spreading of the river plume shown in

Figure 5□suggest that the plume spreads rapidly offshore. How far offshore does the plume

propagate under the ice? *Yankovsky and Chapman* [1997] developed a scale-length for the

offshore extent of a buoyant surface-advected plume for a *steady* outflow in the absence of

surface friction:

$$y_s = \frac{2\left(3g'h_o + v_i^2\right)}{f\left(2g'h_o + v_i^2\right)^{1/2}}$$

where y_s is the offshore extent of the plume, $g' = g\Delta\rho/\rho_o$ and v_i is the inflow velocity, h_o is the

inflow depth, and f is the Coriolis parameter (1.37 x 10^{-4} s^{-1} at 71°N). Although the steady-

state, inviscid assumptions do not strictly apply to the impulsive-type discharge characteristic of arctic rivers in early summer or for plumes under landfast ice (where friction might be important), we nevertheless apply this theory to early June when the peak outflow of the Kuparuk River is about 2000 m^3-s^{-1}. We take the effective width of the river mouth to be 1 km and the inflow depth to be 2 m, so that $v_i \sim 1.1$ m-s^{-1}. From the salinity cross-section, we estimate $\Delta\rho \sim 22$ kg-m^{-3}, $\rho_o \sim 1025$ kg-m^{-3} so that $g' \sim 0.21$ m^2- s^{-2}. For these values the offshore extent of the plume is ~25 km and well beyond the region of our measurements. The plume might in fact extend further offshore because of frictional coupling between the plume and ice. Nevertheless, for the case considered, the propagation speed of a gravity current is

$c = \sqrt{2g'h_o}$ [*Benjamin*, 1968], so that $c \sim 0.9$ m-s^{-1} for the assumed parameters. Hence the plume should propagate the distance y_s in less than a day. Note also that *Yankovsky and Chapman's* scaling assume no ambient mean flow. Our observations indicate that the spring freshet can occur during periods of variable along-shelf flow and these might alter the offshore distance that the buoyant river plume can spread [*Yankovsky*, in press].

Stratification also affects the velocity profile as shown by the mean open water season profiles from REINDEER (**Figure 54** □□**55**□ Similar to **Figure**□□ □□ □□ the means are computed separately for westward and eastward flow events and plotted versus the scaled depth to account for changes in water column depth.

When the along-shore flow is eastward (**Figure 54**), there is little shear in the along- and cross-shore velocities. Eastward currents occur under eastward or downwelling favorable winds, which (at steady state and under an idealized two-dimensional case) cause offshore transport of low density water in the bottom boundary layer. As this water flows seaward it convectively mixes with denser surface water to rapidly erode stratification. The breakdown in stratification allows the efficient vertical transport of vertical momentum from the wind throughout the water column leading to small velocity shears and, if the water column is sufficiently shallow, overlapping of the surface and bottom Ekman layers. Interestingly, we do not observe onshore transport in the surface layer and offshore transport in the bottom for eastward flow (left panel of **Figure 54**) for this downwelling case. There are several possible reasons for this. First, our simple averaging approach might mask bottom Ekman layers. Second, a sufficiently strong alongshore pressure gradient would force an onshore geostrophic flow that swamps the Ekman transport. Lastly, the shelf flow field is likely three-dimensional, so that our simple two-dimensional analysis cannot be applied to this setting.

For westward or upwelling favorable winds the mean flow is westward (right panel of **Figure 55**), but the velocity profile is highly sheared. The sheared structure is consistent with surface offshore transport of low-density water and onshore transport of denser water beneath the surface layer. In aggregate these effects tend to enhance stratification, which in turn, inhibits vertical mixing of momentum. Thus a shallow surface Ekman layer forms wherein the wind momentum is confined to the surface layer (e.g., above the pycnocline depth). Hence the along-shore flow is substantially greater at the surface than below the pycnocline. While we do not have measurements of the stratification throughout the open water period, the mean velocity shear in **Figure 55** suggests that the depth of the pycnocline during upwelling conditions in July and August 2002 is at about $1 - 2$ m. We note that the difference in speeds and velocity structure are not due to the winds being stronger to the west than to the east during the 2002 open water season. In fact, the mean wind stress is strongly eastward during this season (**Figure** ☐) although these did not cause swifter surface velocities than those observed under the weaker westward wind stress. An understanding of the asymmetric response to upwelling and downwelling favorable winds in the presence of stratification is extremely important for understanding the regional circulation field.

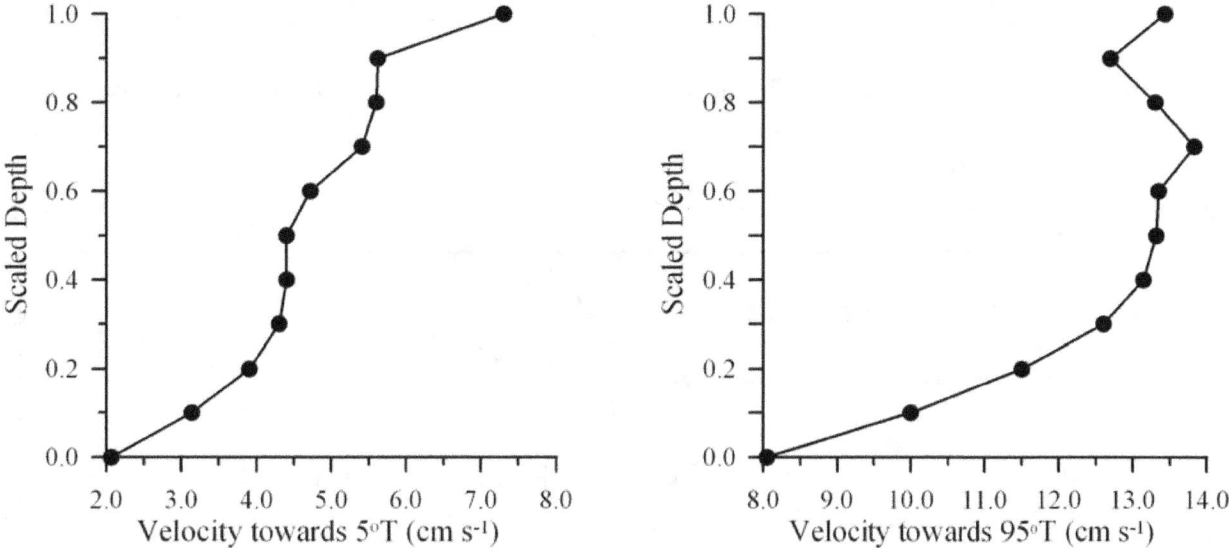

Figure 54. Mean velocity profiles for the cross-shore (left) and alongshore (right) velocity components during eastward flow conditions at REINDEER for the open water season.

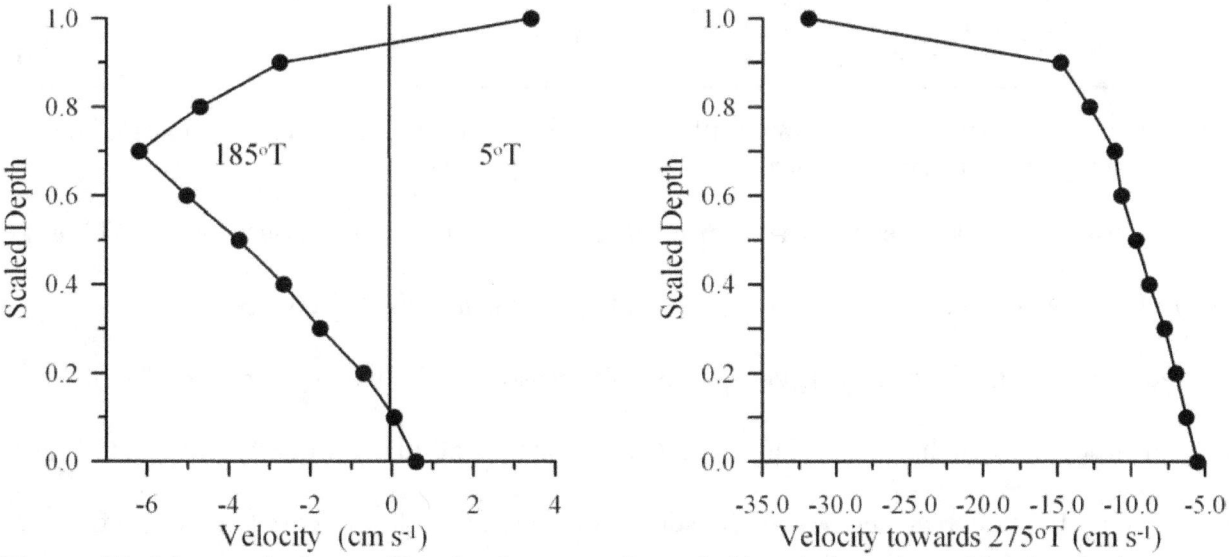

Figure 55. Mean velocity profiles for the cross-shore (left) and alongshore (right) velocity components during westward flow conditions at REINDEER for the open water season.

The character of the plume is expected to change seasonally, as shown schematically in **Figure 5**⬜from the shallow, strongly-stratified and surface-advected plume (red) of early summer to the bottom-advected plume type of late summer and fall (blue). The latter develops

91

in late summer and fall after mixing has destroyed the stratification and likely includes a swift alongshore geostrophic flow embedded within the front that can carry materials eastward along the Alaskan coast. Moreover the front effectively blocks cross-shelf transport and so materials shoreward of the front tend to remain trapped there unless the flow is interrupted by upwelling winds and/or frontal instabilities.

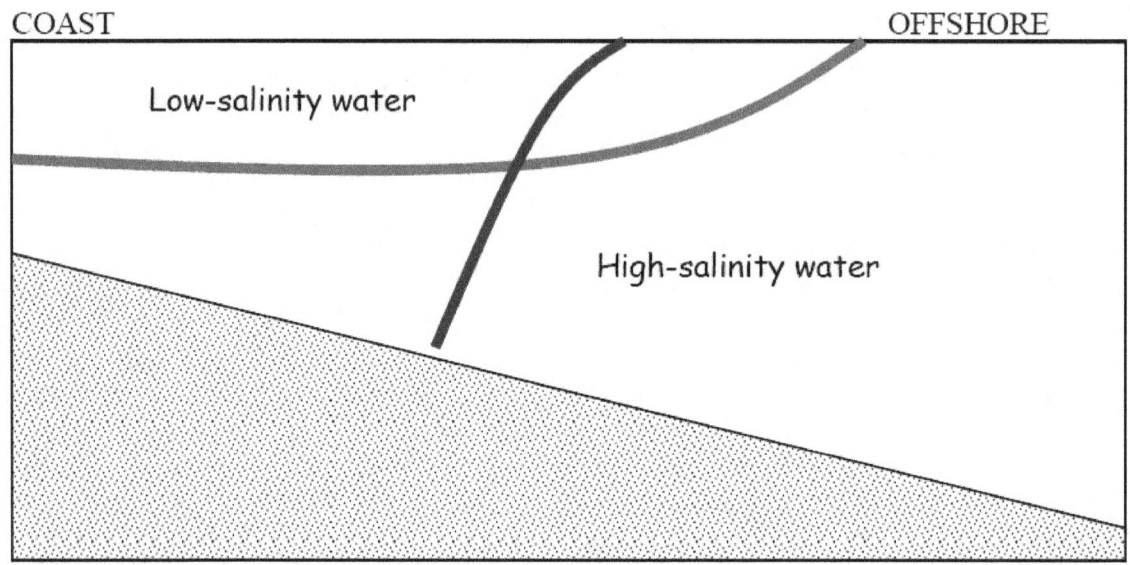

Figure 56. Schematic of the freshwater plume types likely to form in summer and fall in the nearshore region of the Beaufort Sea.

Instabilities have been observed in satellite images of the Alaskan Beaufort Sea (**Figures 57 and 58**). Although not directly wind-driven, the frontal structure and hence the characteristics of the instability do depend upon the seasonal wind history as these affect the frontal structure through mixing. The images show tongues of turbid water extending from near the coast to the shelfbreak and beyond (in some cases more than 100 km offshore). The flow in these unstable plumes has not been measured in the Alaskan Beaufort Sea. However, *Weingartner et al.* [1999] sampled similar features associated with the buoyancy-forced Siberian Coastal Current in the Chukchi Sea and found cross-shore velocities of up to 30 cm-s^{-1}. Thus, instabilities could rapidly transport materials and pollutants from the nearshore Beaufort Sea offshore and possibly, based on these images, across the shelfbreak and along the major fall

migration corridor for bowhead whales.

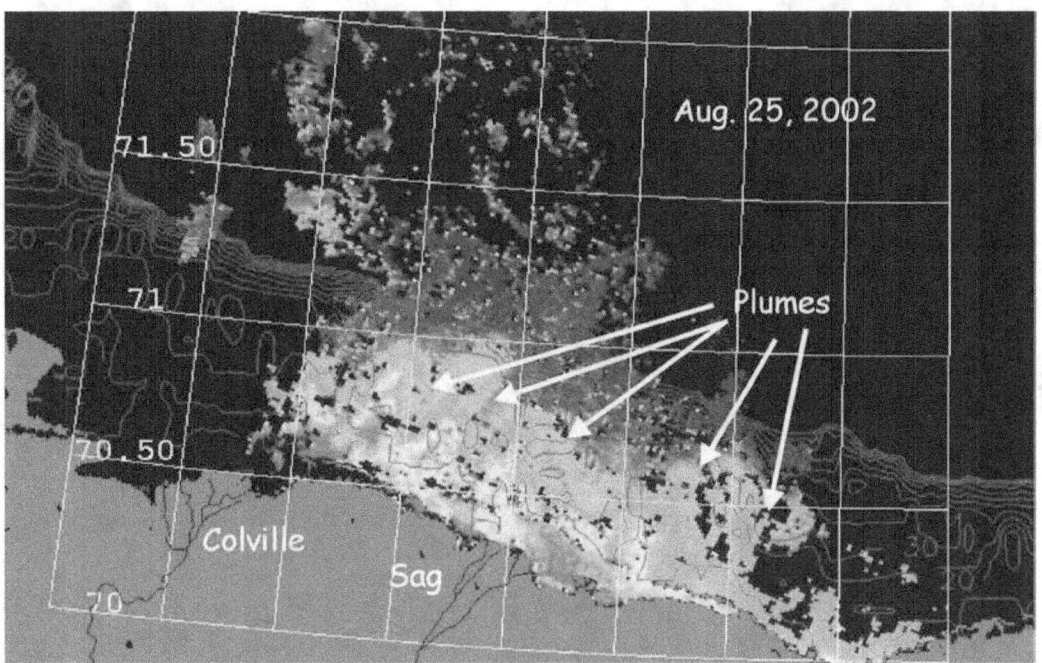

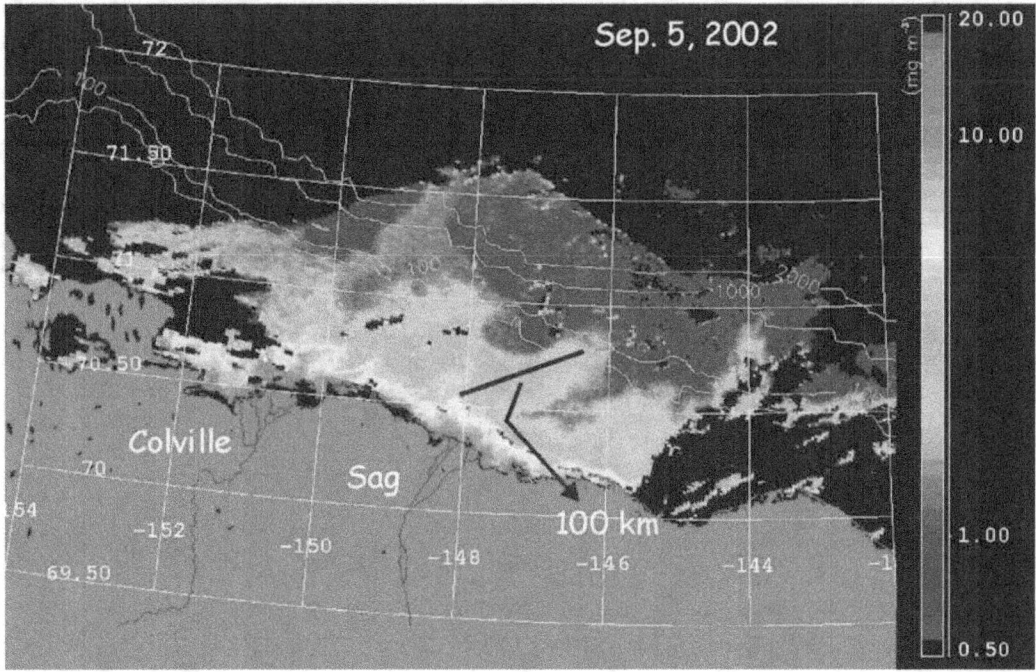

Figure 5 Beaufort Sea SeaWIFS imagery from August 25, 2002 (upper panel) and September 5, 2002 (lower panel). Winds were weak and variable for the week preceding these images.

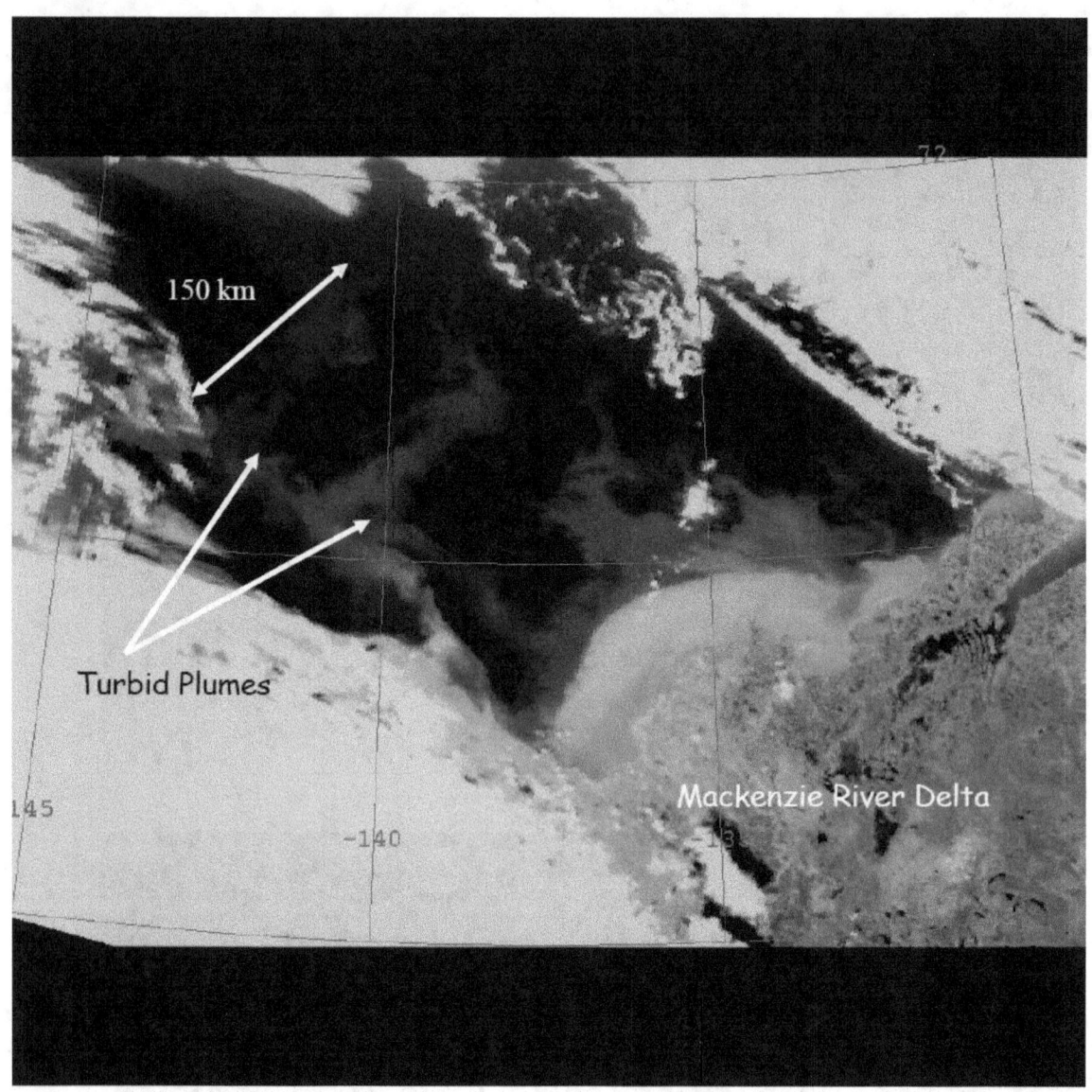

Figure 58. Visible SeaWIFS image from September 4, 2004 showing turbid plumes extending seaward from the Alaskan Beaufort Sea shelf across the continental slope.

Three years of current meter and water property measurements were made in the nearshore region of the Alaskan Beaufort Sea to assess circulation dynamics of the region beneath the landfast ice. The measurements, made within Stefannsson Sound show a distinct seasonal cycle associated with the formation and ablation of the landfast ice.

The mean flow, whether averaged over the entire record or by season, is small and in seldom significantly different from zero. It is, however, highly variable in time with the dominant mode of variability being in the along-shore direction. During the open water season the currents are swift ($10 - 50$ cm-s^{-1}), strongly sheared, especially when the flow is westward, and significantly correlated with the winds. During the landfast ice season currents are small (generally ~ 5 cm-s^{-1}), weakly sheared, and uncorrelated with winds. Nevertheless, the winter sub-tidal flow variance implies fluctuating along-shore sea level gradients of $O(10^{-6})$. The origin of these sea-level slopes is not known. Measurements now being made under MMS support are focused on directly measuring the along-shore pressure and velocity fields in order to identify the possible origins of these gradients and to investigate the regional momentum balance. We further recommend that simple idealized numerical model studies be conducted to examine the origins of the underice forcing and its affects on the underice flow field.

Freshwater discharge associated with the springtime freshet creates shallow, strongly stratified, underice plumes that likely spread up to 20 km or more offshore. The cross-shore flows associated with these plume can be as large as 10 cm-s^{-1} and are much larger than the cross-shore flows generally observed beneath the landfast ice in winter. Little is known about these plumes, although they provide a vehicle by which nearshore suspended and dissolved materials can be carried offshore by spreading of the plume beneath the ice, offshore Ekman

95

transport (once the ice breaks up), or through frontal instabilities. The latter generate large cross-shelf plumes that can extend across the Beaufort shelf and slope. Measurements obtained from similar features in the Chukchi Sea indicate that cross-shelf velocities associated with these instabilities can be ~25 cm-s^{-1}. We recommend that measurements be conducted to quantify the flow within these cross-shore jets and to determine the mechanisms by which they are generated. MMS is currently supporting nearshore measurements using shore-based, high-frequency radar. We urge that shipboard sampling be made in conjunction with the radar measurements to identify the characteristics (stratification, plume thickness) of these jets and the mechanisms that generate them.

Stratification due to freshwater inflow leads to a strong asymmetric response in the velocity shear between upwelling (westward winds) and downwelling (eastward) conditions on the inner shelf. Westward surface flows are intensified during upwelling events because the wind's momentum is trapped to a strongly stratified surface layer, while eastward surface currents are weaker during downwelling because stratification is weaker and the momentum from the surface stress is mixed over a deeper layer. The results imply that circulation models must correctly incorporate runoff and stratification in order to reproduce the surface circulation field correctly. Observations on the seasonal evolution of the open water stratification structure are needed to better understand this asymmetry and for model evaluations.

The seasonal cycle in sediment transport likely consists of rapid deposition from the freshwater plume as it spreads beneath the sea ice followed by several re-suspension events during the open water season. Upon re-suspension, sediments can be advected offshore within the coastal flows or carried offshore due to instabilities. Re-suspension also appears to be prominent during freeze-up and we presume that much sediment is incorporated into the landfast ice at this time. This sediment will then remain in the landfast ice matrix until the ice break-ups and drifts away the following summer or will drop out during ice melt.

Our data suggest that oil is unlikely to be carried far in the event of a spill beneath the landfast ice. Instead the oil will be transported back and forth along the coast. If the *Cox and Schmidt* [1980] laboratory measurements apply to this region of the Beaufort Sea, then oil will not move far once it has attained its equilibrium slick thickness. In the event of an underice spill here, the rate and direction of the spreading oil can be monitored because the current field is spatially coherent over at least 30 km in the alongshore direction. Thus a single current meter can be lowered through a hole in the ice and transmit current data in real-time to the spill recovery team. Direct measurements are required because of the absence of a significant wind-current correlation in winter.

Oil spilled beneath the ice during the spring freshet could be carried offshore of Stefansson Sound within the underice river plume. Application of theories developed for mid-latitude settings on the offshore extent of a river plume discharged into the sea suggests that oil might be carried at least 20 km offshore during the spring freshet. These theories do not consider the possibly complex frictional coupling between the ice and flow field or the impulsive nature of arctic river discharges. We recommend that theoretical and observational studies be conducted in the Alaskan Beaufort Sea directed at understanding the underice spreading of river plumes. We believe that the current measuring techniques developed in this project can be applied to such a study.

Oil adsorbed onto sediments provides another mechanism for the dispersal of this pollutant. Some of the sediments are transported by the currents and some by the sea ice, although it is not known how the load is partitioned between the two. The sediment load in ice

97

can be easily determined from ice cores collected in spring prior to break-up. The fate of the landfast ice can then be determined by deploying satellite tracked drifters in the ice prior to break-up. Once the ice begins to break-up its drift and subsequent melt can be ascertained with the aid of the drifters.

The complex deformation field of the landfast ice regime suggests that frictional coupling between ice and currents will vary substantially over the shelf covered by landfast ice due to both skin and form drag, which are functions of both the underice topography and flow field [*McPhee*, 1990]. Measurements and models are required to quantify this frictional coupling. Mapping of underice topography should be conducted several times per winter and cover a variety of along- and cross-shore spatial scales. The larger scales can be mapped efficiently using airborne electromagnetic sensors or laser profilometry, whereas smaller scales will require ground-based measurements.

Based upon preliminary numerical modeling activities, it appears that there is little exchange between waters beneath the landfast ice and those offshore. This topic needs further exploration using models and observations. One integrated observational approach that is relatively simple to undertake is to measure the $\delta^{18}O$ fraction in ice cores in spring after the ice reaches its maximum thickness. Since this isotope ratio is substantially different between sea-water and river water, spring ice cores will precisely record when the river water was exhausted from the nearshore region [*Macdonald et al.*, 1999b]. This will lead to a distinct horizon in the ice core of the isotope ratio transition. The timing of the transition can be determined by calculating ice growth rate from coastal meteorological data. This is a relatively inexpensive procedure that would provide a measure of year-to-year differences in the rate of freshwater depletion from the nearshore Beaufort Sea after the landfast ice forms.

ACKNOWLEDGMENTS

We are grateful for the financial support provided by the Minerals Management Service, the equipment provided by the Alaska Department of Environmental Conservation, and logistical support from BP, Inc. We thank Dave Leech for his expertise in designing and deploying the moorings and for his cheerful approach throughout the project. John Trefey assisted with the 2001 CTD measurements. G. Michael Schmidt kindly processed the SeaWIFS images.

REFERENCES

Aagaard, K., The Beaufort Undercurrent. IN: *The Alaskan Beaufort Sea: Ecosystems and Environment*, edited by P. W. Barnes, D. M. Schell, and E. Reimnitz, pp. 47-71. Academic Press, New York, 1984.

Aagaard, K., and A.T. Roach, Arctic ocean-shelf exchange: Measurements in Barrow Canyon, *J. Geophys. Res.*, *95*, 18163-18175, 1990.

Barnes, P. W., D. M. Rearic, and E. Reimnitz, Ice gouging characteristics and processes IN: *The Alaskan Beaufort Sea: Ecosystems and Environment*, edited by P. W. Barnes, D. M. Schell, and E. Reimnitz, pp. 185 - 212. Academic Press, New York, 1984.

Barnes and Reimnitz, 1974 IN The Coast and Shelf of the Beaufort Sea (JC Reed and J E Sater, eds.) p. 439, Arctic Institute of North America, Arlington, VA. 1974

Benjamin, T. B., Gravity currents and related phenomena, *J. Fluid Mech., 31, (2),* 209 – 248, 1968

Brower, W. A., Jr., R. G. Baldwin, C. N. Williams, Jr., J. L .Wise, and L.D. Leslie, *Climate atlas of the outer continental shelf waters and coastal regions of Alaska, volume III, Chukchi-Beaufort Sea*, 497 pp., National Climatic Data Center, Asheville, NC, 28801, 1988.

Carmack, E. C., R. W. Macdonald, and J. E. Papdakis, Water mass structure and boundaries in the Mackenzie Shelf Estuary, *J. Geophys. Res., 94*, 18043-18055, 1989.

Chapman, D. C. and S. J. Lentz, Trapping of a coastal density front by the bottom boundary layer, *J. Phys. Oceanogr., 24*, 1464-1479, 1994.

Colonell, J. M. and B. J. Galloway, Wind-driven transport and dispersion of age-0 arctic ciscoes along the Alaska Beaufort coast. IN: *Fish Ecology in Arctic North America*, American Fisheries Society Symposium 19, Bethesda, MD., p – 90 – 103, 1997.

Cox, J. C. and I. A. Schultz, The transport and behavior of spilled oil under ice. Proceedings of the Third Annual Technical Seminar, Arctic Marine Oil Spill Program, Edmonton, June 1979, p. 45 – 61, 1980.

Csanady, G. T. Circulation in the Coastal Ocean, D. Reidel, Boston, p. 279, 1982.

Danielson, S. L. and Z. Kowalik, Tidal currents in the St. Lawrence Island region. *J. Geophys. Res.*, in press.

Dean, K. G., W. Stringer, K. Ahlnaes, S.C. Searcy, and T. Weingartner, The influence of river discharge on the thawing of sea ice: Mackenzie River Delta: Albedo and temperature analysis, *Polar Res., 13*, 83-94, 1994.

Dunton, K. H., E. Reimnitz, and S. V. Schonberg, An arctic kelp community in the Alaskan Beaufort Sea, *Arctic, 35*: 465 – 484., 1982.

Denman, K. L. and M. Miyake, Upper layer modification at ocean station Papa: observations and simulation, *J. Phys. Oceanogr.*, 3, 185 – 196, 1973.

Guay, C. K. and K. K. Falkner, A survey of dissolved barium in the estuaries of major Arctic rivers and adjacent seas. *Cont. Shelf Res., 8:* 859 – 882, 1998.

Foreman, M. G.G. Manual for Tidal Currents Analysis and Prediction. Pacific Marine Science Report 78-6, Institute of Ocean Sciences, Patricia Bay, Sidney, B.C., 1978, 70 pp.

Furey, P., The large-scale surface wind field over the western Arctic Ocean, 1981 – 1993, MS thesis, 121 pp. Univ. of Alaska, Fairbanks, 1998

Kowalik, Z. and A. Y. Proshutinsky, The Arctic Ocean Tides, in *The Polar Oceans and Their Role in Shaping the Global Environment; Geophys. Monogr. 85,* pp. 137-158, edited by O. M. Johannessen, R. D. Muench and J. E. Overland, Amer. Geophys. Union, Washington, DC, 1994.

Kozo, T. L., An observational study of sea breezes along the Alaska Beaufort Sea coast, *J. Appl. Met. 21*: 891- 905, 1982a.

Kozo, T. L., An mathematical model of sea breezes along the Alaska Beaufort Sea coast, *J. Appl.* Met. 21: 906 - 924, 1982b.

Kozo, T. L. Mesoscale wind phenomena along the Alaskan Beaufort Sea coast. IN: *The Alaskan Beaufort Sea: Ecosystems and Environment*, edited by P. Barnes and E. Reimnitz, pp. 23 - 45. Academic Press, New York, 1984.

Kozo, T. L. Mountain barrier baroclinicity effects on surface winds along the Alaskan Arctic coast. *Geophys. Res. Lett.*, 7, 377 – 380, 1980.

Lentz, S. J. Current dynamics over the northern California inner shelf, *J. Phys. Oceanogr.*, 24, 2461 – 2478, 1994.

Lentz, S., R. T. Guza, S. Elgar, F. Fedderesen, and T.H. C. Herbers, Momentum balances on the North Carolina inner shelf, *J. Geophys. Res.,* 104, 18205 – 18226, 1999.

Macdonald, R.W., E.C. Carmack, F. A. McLaughlin, K. K. Falkner, and J. H. Swift, Connections among ice, runoff, and atmospheric forcing in the Beaufort Gyre, *Geophys. Res. Lett.,* 26:15:2223 – 2226, 1999a.

MacDonald, R. W., E. C. Carmack, and D. W. Paton. Using the delta ^{18}O composition in landfast ice as a record of arctic estuarine processes. *Mar. Chem.* 65: 3 – 24, 1999b.

Macdonald, R.W., E.C. Carmack, F. A. McLaughlin, K. Iseki, D.M. Macdonald, and M. C. O'Brien, Composition and Modification of water masses in the Mackenzie Shelf Estuary, *J. Geophys. Res., 94*, 18057-18070, 1989.

Macdonald, R. W. and E. C. Carmack, The role of large-scale under-ice topography in separating estuary and ocean on an arctic shelf. *Atmosphere-Ocean, 29*: 37 -51, 1991.

Matthews, J.B., Observations of Under-ice circulation in a shallow lagoon in the Alaskan Beaufort Sea, *Ocean Management*, 6, 223-234, 1981.

Maslanik, J. A., M. A. Serreze, and T. Agnew, On the record reduction in 1998 Western Arctic Sea ice cover, *Geophys. Res. Lett.*, 26, 1905 – 1908, 1999.

Maykut, G. A. The surface heat and mass balance, IN: *The Geophysics of Sea Ice*, edited by N. Untersteiner, pp. 395 -464, Plenum Press, New York, NY, 1986.

McPhee, M. G., Small-Scale Processes. IN: *Polar Oceaongraphy Part A: Physical Science*, edited by W. O. Smith, Jr., pp. 287 - 280. Academic Press, New York, 1990.

Morris, K., S. Li, and M. Jefferies, Meso- and microscale sea-ice motion in the East Siberian Sea as determined from ERS-1 SAR data. *J. Glaciol.,* 45(15): 370 – 383, 1999.

Mountain, D. G., Coachman, L. K., and K. Aagaard, On the flow through Barrow Canyon, *J. Phys. Oceanogr.* 6, 461 – 470, 1976.

North, G. R., T. L. Bell, and R. F. Cahalan, Sampling Errors in the estimation of empirical orthogonal functions, *Monthly Weath. Rev., 110,* 699-706, 1982

Pawlowicz, R., B. Beardsley, and S. Lentz. Classical tidal harmonic analysis including error estimates in MATLAB using T.TIDE, *Comp. and Geosci.,* 28, 929- 937, 2002.

Pickart, R. S. Shelbreak circulation in the Alaskan Beaufort Sea: Mean structure and variability, *J. Geophys. Res.,* 2004.

Pickart, R.S., T. Weingartner, L.J. Pratt, S. Zimmermann, and D. J. Torres, Flow of winter-transformed Pacific water into the western Arctic (accepted, Deep-Sea Research)

Reimnitz, E., Interaction of river discharge with sea ice in proximity of Arctic deltas: a review, *Polarforschung,* 70: 123 – 134, 2000.

Reimnitz, E. and E. W. Kempema, Pack ice interaction with stamukhi shoal. IN: The Alaskan Beaufort Sea: Ecosystems and Environment, edited by P. W. Barnes, D. M. Schell, and E. Reimnitz, pp. 159 - 184. Academic Press, New York, 1984.

Searcy, C., K. Dean, and W. Stringer, A river-coastal sea ice interaction model: Mackenzie River Delta, *J. Geophys. Res., 101,* 8885-8894, 1996.

Tucker III, W. B., W. F. Weeks, and M. Frank, Sea Ice ridging over the Alaskan continental shelf, *J. Geophys. Res., 84,* 4885 – 4897, 1979.

Weingartner, T., K. Aagaard, R. Woodgate, S. Danielson, Y. Sasaki, D. Cavalieri, Circulation on the North Central Chukchi Sea Shelf (accepted, Deep-Sea Research)

Weingartner, T.J., S. Danielson, Y. Sasaki, V. Pavlov, and M. Kulakov, The Siberian Coastal Current: A wind- and buoyancy-forced arctic coastal current, *J. Geophys. Res.,* 104, 29697-29713, 1999.

Weingartner, T.J., D.J. Cavalieri, K. Aagaard, and Y. Sasaki, Circulation, dense water formation, and outflow on the northeast Chukchi shelf, *J. Geophys. Res., 103,* 7647-7661, 1998.

Wiseman et al., W.J., Suhayda, J.N., Hus, S.A., and Walters, C.D., IN The Coast and Shelf of the Beaufort Sea (JC Reed and J E Sater, eds.) p. 49, Arctic Institute of North America, Arlington, VA. 1974

Woodgate, R. A., K. Aagaard, and T. Weingartner. A year in the physical oceanography of the Chukchi Sea: Moored measurements from autumn 1990-91. (accepted, Deep-Sea Research).

Yankovsky, A. Interaction of transient shelf currents with a buoyancy-driven coastal current. *J. Geophys. Res.,* (in press).

Yankovsky, A. E. and D. C. Chapman, A simple theory for the fate of buoyant coastal discharges, *J. Phys. Oceanogr., 27,* 1386-1401, 1997.

The Department of the Interior Mission

As the Nation's principal conservation agency, the Department of the Interior has responsibility for most of our nationally owned public lands and natural resources. This includes fostering sound use of our land and water resources; protecting our fish, wildlife, and biological diversity; preserving the environmental and cultural values of our national parks and historical places; and providing for the enjoyment of life through outdoor recreation. The Department assesses our energy and mineral resources and works to ensure that their development is in the best interests of all our people by encouraging stewardship and citizen participation in their care. The Department also has a major responsibility for American Indian reservation communities and for people who live in island territories under U.S. administration.

The Minerals Management Service Mission

As a bureau of the Department of the Interior, the Minerals Management Service's (MMS) primary responsibilities are to manage the mineral resources located on the Nation's Outer Continental Shelf (OCS), collect revenue from the Federal OCS and onshore Federal and Indian lands, and distribute those revenues.

Moreover, in working to meet its responsibilities, the ☐☐☐☐re ☐i☐er☐☐☐ ☐☐ge☐e☐☐☐r☐gr☐☐ administers the OCS competitive leasing program and oversees the safe and environmentally sound exploration and production of our Nation's offshore natural gas, oil and other mineral resources. The MMS ☐☐☐☐☐☐ ☐ ☐☐ge☐e☐☐☐r☐gr☐☐ meets its responsibilities by ensuring the efficient, timely and accurate collection and disbursement of revenue from mineral leasing and production due to Indian tribes and allottees, States and the U.S. Treasury.

The MMS strives to fulfill its responsibilities through the general guiding principles of: (1) being responsive to the public's concerns and interests by maintaining a dialogue with all potentially affected parties and (2) carrying out its programs with an emphasis on working to enhance the quality of life for all Americans by lending MMS assistance and expertise to economic development and environmental protection.